AF013

MASSIMILIANO AFIERO

AXIS FORCES 13

WW2 AXIS FORCES

The Axis Forces 013 - First edition February 2020 by Luca Cristini Editor for the brand Soldiershop
Cover & Art Design by soldiershop factory.   ISBN code: 978-88-93275583
Copyright © 2020 Luca Cristini Editore (BG) ITALY.   No part of this publication may be reproduced, stored in a retrieval system or transmitted by any form or by any means, electronic, recording or otherwise without the prior permission in writing from the publishers. The publisher remains to disposition of the possible having right for all the doubtful sources images or not identifies.
Visit www.soldiershop.com to read more about all our books and to buy them.

The Axis Forces Number 13 – February 2020

Direction and editing: Via San Giorgio, 11 – 80021 Afragola (NA) - ITALIA
Managing and Chief Editor: Massimiliano Afiero
Email: maxafiero@libero.it - **Website:** www.maxafiero.it

Contributors

Tomasz Borowski, Grégory Bouysse, Stefano Canavassi, Carlos Caballero Jurado, Rene Chavez, Gary Costello, Paolo Crippa, Carlo Cucut, Antonio Guerra, John B. Köser, Lars Larsen, Christophe Leguérandais, Eduardo M. Gil Martínez, Michael D. Miller, Peter Mooney, Péter Mujzer, Ken Niewiarowicz, Erik Norling, Raphael Riccio, Marc Rikmenspoel, Samcevich Andrei, Charles Trang, Cesare Veronesi, Sergio Volpe

Editorial

Here is finally the first issue of our magazine of 2020, also released this time overcoming a thousand logistical problems to select and complete the layout of the articles in close collaboration with the various authors spread all over the world. As always, we hope to have chosen interesting topics for our new articles, to meet the requests of our ever-increasing readers. Our main field of interest also for this new year will focus on Axis formations in World War II, with an eye to volunteer formations made up of foreign personnel. In the next issues we will also continue to follow the various anniversaries of the battles and campaigns of 1940, starting from the campaign on the Western Front, to the entry into the war of Italy, to continue with the campaign in North Africa, East Africa and the invasion of Greece. We naturally need the help and collaboration of everyone, so we always invite you to send us comments and critiques on our articles and on any topics you would like to be treated in greater depth. Let's now take a look the contents of this new issue: let's start with an article dedicated to the use of the SS Prinz Eugen division during the 'Schwarz' operation, conducted on the Balkan front in May 1943. This is followed by the biography of Philipp Theiss, extracted from the new book by our Peter Mooney. We continue with the first part of the article dedicated to the recruitment of the Cossacks into the German armed forces and with the second part of the monumental work dedicated to the Krüger brothers by our Mike Miller. Finally, we close with an equally voluminous work on foreign nurses who served in the German Red Cross, a topic little treated by official historiography. Happy reading to all and see you next issue.

Massimiliano Afiero

The publication of The Axis Forces deals exclusively with subjects of a historical military nature and is not intended to promote any type of political ideology either present or past, as it also does not seek to exalt any type of political regime of the past century or any form of racism.

Contents

Operation Schwarz: May 1944. The Prinz Eugen in action!	Pag. 5
SS-Haupsturmführer Philipp Theiss	Pag. 24
Hitler's Cossacks	Pag. 30
The SS Generals Walter and Friedrich-Wilhelm Krüger, part 2	Pag. 37
«While I can walk, I will stay». Awarded foreign DRK-nurses	Pag. 58

Operation Schwarz: May 1944
The Prinz Eugen in action!
by Massimiliano Afiero

SS-Ostubaf. **Heinrich Petersen.**

In early May 1943, the *SS-Frw.Geb.Div. 'Prinz Eugen'* was subordinated to *Heeresgruppe E* for employment in western Montenegro in a new anti-partisan operation called *Schwarz*, in cooperation with Italian, Bulgarian and Croatian forces. In Yugoslav historiography, the operation is known as the Battle of Sutjeska. The objective was to wipe out Tito's forces that had been able to withdraw to Montenegro after Operation *Weiss*. Once again, however, Tito was able to break out of the encirclement and lead the remnants of his Popular Army to Bosnia, crossing the Sutjeska River. On the German side, the forces employed were the *Prinz Eugen*, the *1.Gebirgs-Division*, the *104.Jäger-Division*, the *118.Jäger-Division*, the *369.Kro.Infanterie-Division*, personnel of the special units of the *Brandenburg* Regiment, and *Infanterie-Regiment 724* of the *104.Infanterie-Division*. The *Prinz Eugen* units began to move on May 15. *SS-Geb.Jg.Rgt 1*, which as of April 16, 1943, had been commanded by *SS-Ostubaf.* Heinrich Petersen[1], advancing from the area southeast of Mostar, reached the eastern side of Blagaj with its *II.Battalion* without having to engage in any fighting. The *8.Kompanie* took about a hundred prisoners outside of Mostar. It was not until late in the morning that several firefights erupted along the road to the east of Blagaj. *SS-Geb.Jg.Rgt 2* meanwhile was engaged in an attack against Nevesinje, without sustaining any significant losses. On May 16, Bilece was reached after having crossed the

The Axis Forces

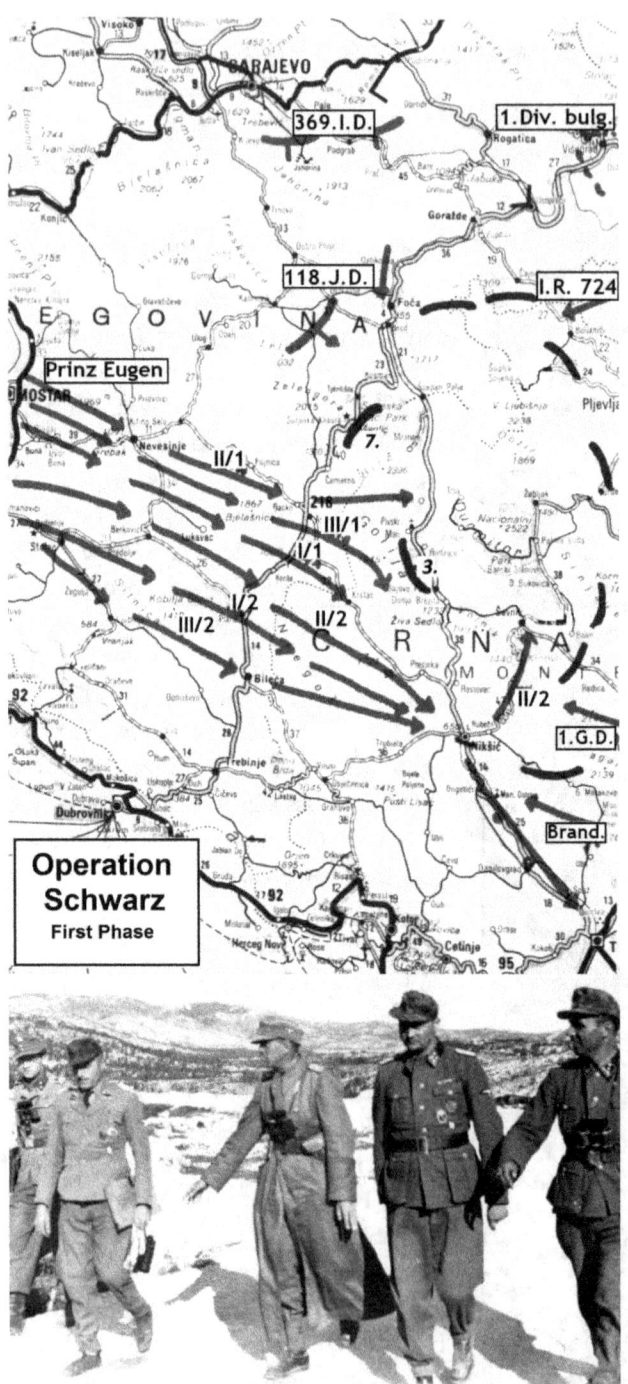

Operation Schwarz
First Phase

From the left, *SS-Stubaf.* Hahn, *SS-Gruf.* Phleps, *SS-Ostubaf.* Petersen and *SS-Ostuf.* Niedermeier.

Fatnica Plain. On May 20, *I./SS-Geb.Jg.Rgt 2* reached Niksic without encountering any partisan units. The same day, however, units of *SS-Geb.Jg.Rgt 1* were engaged against enemy formations that were fighting as they fell back; *I.Battalion* under *SS-Stubaf.* Herbert Vollmer[2] reached Stepen, southeast of Mostar, while the other two battalions of the regiment were to the east of the Avtovac-Cemerno road. At that time the Corps ordered an offensive thrust against Podgorica, where strong partisan units had been able to pass through the Italian lines, inflicting significant losses. Accordingly, a combat group to seal the gap was formed consisting of *III./SS-Geb.Jg.Rgt 2*, a battery of artillery from the regiment, the armored company, two *Flak* platoons and an engineer platoon. At the same time, the headquarters of the Italian *Ferrara* Division at Nikisc reported to Phleps that two enemy brigades were to the north of Nikisc, around Savnik. Assistance was requested from the air force, which shortly thereafter hit positions around Savnik and Zabljak, where the largest concentrations of enemy forces had been spotted. Towards evening, *Kampfgruppe Meckelburg* arrived and made contact with the enemy. *SS-Ostubaf.* Petersen was busy fighting other enemy units: *I./SS-Geb.Jg.Rgt 1* found itself caught up in fighting as it advanced towards Gornje Polje, southwest of Savnik. *II./SS-Geb.Jg.Rgt 1*, meanwhile, was engaged in the area of Jasenovo Polje, further to the north, in bitter fighting. Thanks to radio intercepts and information gained from prisoners, the location of enemy units was discovered: the 1st Proletarian Division was marching towards the east, west of Lim, the 2nd Proletarian Division was southwest of the Niksic-Podgorica area, and the 3rd Division was on the line Avtovac-Niksic and in contact with the 7th Division north of Sutjeska. Other units, along with Tito's staff, were on the outskirts of Zabljac. The intention of the partisan forces was to cross the Lim and to advance into southern Serbia.

A *Prinz Eugen* motorcycle unit passing through a Bosnian village.

Gebirgsjägers climbing a mountain in search of the enemy during Operation "*Schwarz*".

A *Prinz Eugen* French *Somua S-35*, designated in German as the *PzKpfw 35-S 739(f)*.

The British had furnished radio equipment to Tito, but German intelligence had managed to decipher the rebel message traffic and discover their plans. Facing the concentration of enemy forces along the Lim in the direction of Durmitor were units of *1.Gebirgs-Division* and a regiment from *Brandenburg*. Further to the north was *Gruppe Ludwiger* of the *104. Jäger-Division*, while to the left of *1.Geb.Div.* were units of *Prinz Eugen* with their right flank to the north passing through Nikisc. *SS-Geb.Jg.Rgt 1* was still committed to attacking to the southeast. The *369.Kroatische-Infanterie-Division* was in the Sarajevo area, while two Bulgarian

The Axis Forces

Gebirgsjägers descending a mountain using a difficult and twisting path.

regiments were in the Visegrad area with the mission of preventing the escape of any partisans to the northeast. The *Prinz Eugen* was ordered to maintain security of the Savnik area, a mission that was assigned to *III./SS-Geb.Jg.Rgt 1*, which was transferred to Nikisc to reinforce the attack force that was already deployed in that sector. *SS-Geb.Jg.Rgt 2* attacked to the east of the Kinsic-Savnik road with Dietsche's II Battalion. Meanwhile, *SS-Geb.Jg.Rgt 1* attacked from the area of Gornje Polje, to the west of the same road.

Fierce fighting

Fierce fighting followed and it was only the commitment of all units to the fight that enabled *SS-Ostubaf.* Petersen to break through along the Gvozd-Gornje Polje line. But it was not over yet; several prisoners revealed that the V Proletarian Brigade was attempting to open a gap in the Orah area, through Gornje Polje. The SS mountain units were thus alerted once again. Another two days of tough fighting followed on the rocky and difficult terrain, but the enemy forces were not able to pass. In the meantime, Dietsche's battalion, ably supported by the *Panzer-Kompanie*, advanced in the direction of Savnik while fighting.

A meeting between Italian and German unit commanders during the operation.

The Axis Forces

SS-Stubaf. Bernhard Dietsche (center) in a discussion with a Chetnik commander, during Operation "*Schwarz*".

The "switchback" road had been cut in several places by the partisans, and it took two days to make it passable again. *SS-Stubaf.* Dietsche attacked the city from the east, encountering stiff resistance. The position was finally captured and the attack continued to the north of the city. For this action, Dietsche was subsequently awarded the Knight's Cross. The last pockets of enemy resistance were eliminated soon after and the last enemy units fell back to the north, towards Durmitor. On May 29, Petersen reached the southern part of the Kormanica Valley, after heavy fighting. Bit by bit, the partisan forces were squeezed around Durmitor. The German command decided to unleash a final attack against the bulk of the enemy forces from the north.

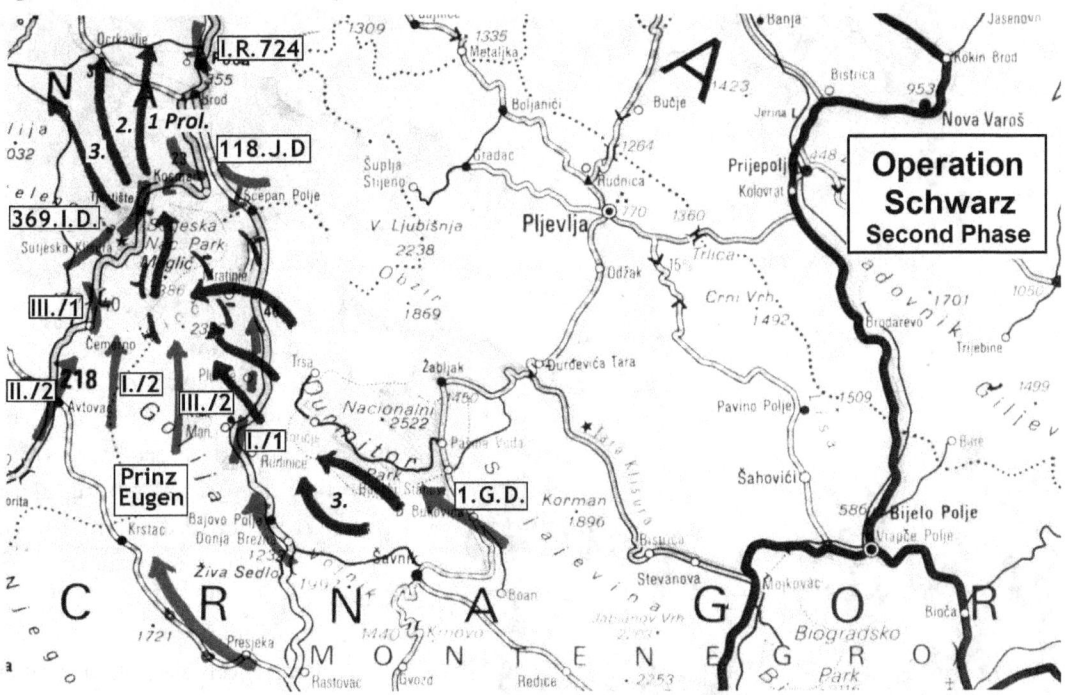

Tito grasped the seriousness of the situation; he had about 40,000 men under his command, but many were wounded or sick. Accordingly, he shifted his weakest units to the east in defensive positions, while he ordered his best unit, the 1st Proletarian Division, to open a gap to the northeast in an attempt to break through the positions of the

118.Jäger-Division or of the *369.Kroatische-Inf.Div*. The first desperate enemy counterattacks fell upon the *118.Jäger-Division* at the confluence of the Piva and Sutjeska Rivers. *II./SS-Geb.Jg.Rgt 1* under *SS-Stubaf*. Hahn on the left flank of the division was also engaged in repulsing the attacks by the partisans. The unit was partially surrounded and it was necessary for *SS-Stubaf*. Biesemeyer and his *Wirtschaft Abteilung* to join in the fighting in order to save the day. Aerial reconnaissance continued to report that the enemy was moving to the north and northwest, and the enemy continued to be pursued closely.

SS soldiers crossing a river.

A *Gebirgsjäger* patrol in the mountains.

From the left, *SS-Ostuf*. Krombholz and *SS-Ostuf*. Grob.

III./SS-Geb.Jg.Rgt 2 was sent in the direction of the Duga gorges, while *II*. advanced along the line Niksic-Bileca and Avtovac. The Italian units advanced toward the Savnik sector, enabling the division to concentrate its efforts on its left flank. SS-Obersturmführer Josef 'Sepp' Krombholz[3], commander of *7.Kompanie*, relates in his diary the responsibilities of Dietsche's II Battalion during this phase: "...*During the main phase of the attack we were loaded onto trucks and moved to the border with Montenegro, without any supplies, pack animals or ammunition reserves. Our commander,* Stubaf. Dietsche, *issued the following order: Maglic had to be taken and the partisan forces defending it had to be wiped out, while the sources of the Piva and the Sutjeska had to be surrounded. To our front the II Battalion of the 1st Regiment was to follow up and support us in the attack against Maglic. The regimental* Streif Kompanie *was to attack on the left in the area of Stabna. The* Streif Kompanie *was not a large unit, having only 180 good troopers. Fighting began around 22:00. We descended the mountain around 2:00. It was completely dark. The descent down the mountain was very difficult.*

Members of the *Prinz Eugen Streif-Kompanie*.

***Prinz Eugen* soldiers.**

***SS-Gebirgsjäger* crossing a stream.**

There was the danger of avalanches. Shots from the enemy were rarely heard. The situation seemed very confused. At 6:00 we had reached the base of the mountain. We began to climb the seven hundred meters of road, heavily laden with weapons and ammunition; to save time, the alpine platoon advanced ahead of us. The others followed closely behind. Around 10:00 the sun disappeared and a squall was imminent. It was good news for us because we would be hidden by the clouds. From the left, in the direction of Stabna, the sound of fighting could be clearly heard, but which ceased after about an hour. Around 11:00 the leading elements of our unit reached the top of the mountain. When all of the units had finally assembled, we moved to the combat zone while encountering little resistance from several partisan units that were retreating. After about ten minutes we reached the first houses of a village. The remains of equipment and uniforms were on the ground, but there were no bodies; perhaps they had already been removed.

Prinz Eugen **motorized column, spring 1943.**

SS-Gebirgsjäger **advancing in an open field to stem the rebel bands, spring 1943.**

Most of the partisan force had pulled back to the eastern side of Maglic. A more thorough reconnaissance had revealed that they had dug in at Livada, a small village two kilometers further west, where they offered strong resistance.

At first we tried to flank the position from the left and then from the right. A frontal attack would have resulted in heavy casualties. There were many partisans. Our commander finally cut to the chase; we and the **Streif Kompanie** *were to attack the area southeast of Maglic to draw out the enemy while the remainder of the forces were to attack them from the rear. The situation was however not easy; the terrain, the fog, and we were without rations for days.*

Tito had managed to assemble many units. Despite the continuous bombardment, the morale of the rebels had not diminished in the least. The next day the 1st Platoon of the 1st Company under Ustuf. *Halbweis, was wiped out while it was searching a gorge.*

Enemy resistance became increasingly intense and a large gap about fifteen kilometers wide had been opened to the east of our regiment's positions. We had to make contact with Staf. *Schmidhuber. We moved through the woods of Maglic towards the northeast, marching in the fog.*

After half a day the leading elements caught up with the tail elements, a sign that we had we had gone around in a circle. It was impossible to get ourselves oriented!".

The division's units were once again assembled on June 1, to be employed in new actions, but most of all to harass the enemy units that were fleeing.

Difficult ascent by an *SS-Gebirgsjäger* unit over rocky karst-like terrain.

SS-Gebirgsjägers **climbing a mountain.**

A *ZB* light machine gun in a firing position.

New operations

After having assembled the units, a new attack was launched to the north. Dietsche's battalion attacked between the battalions of Hahn and of *SS-Stubaf.* Strathmann[4], while it advanced in the direction of Cemerno. Vollmer (*I./SS-Geb.Jg.Rgt 1*), advancing from the south along the course of the Piva River, relieved *Kampfgruppe Hahn*, continuing to advance towards Mratinje to bar crossing the river itself. Schmidhuber assumed command of the northeastern flank of the attack front, with his command post at Krivido. To prevent a possible crossing of the Sutjeska to the west, *III./SS-Geb.Jg.Rgt 1*, commanded by *SS-Ustuf.* Rudolf Bachmann[5], was sent to the west of the river in the Cemerno-Tjentiste sector, while *I./SS-Geb.Jg.Rgt 1* attacked from the south on the other bank of the Sutjeska. The IV Artillery Group provided supporting fire to the two battalions. The fighting in the area between the Piva and Sutjeska Rivers lasted for several days, severely testing the *Prinz Eugen* units. Many partisan forces continued to arrive from the east, crossing the Piva and concentrating in the forests around Javorak. To hamper the arrival of new forces, fierce new attacks were successfully conducted. The *Prinz Eugen* units also found themselves pitted against an enemy brigade, consisting mostly of women who fought very well and with extreme fanaticism.

Prinz Eugen **artillery firing against enemy positions.**

Observing enemy positions.

During the night between 6 and 7 June, the units that were deployed along the Sutjeska were attacked by a fresh enemy brigade, suffering about ten dead and some fifty wounded. The partisans were repulsed, leaving at least two hundred dead on the battlefield. By the end of Operation *Schwarz, the Prinz Eugen* had suffered 112 dead, 424 wounded, and 21 missing in action. With the conclusion of the operation, General Phleps, who had been assigned to command the new *Waffen SS* mountain corps, turned over command of the division to *SS-Brigadeführer* Karl Reichsritter von Oberkamp[6]. Many of the other *Prinz Eugen* officers followed him to assume staff positions in the *V.SS-Gebirgs-Korps*.

SS-Gruf. **Phleps and *SS-Brigadeführer* von Oberkamp at the division command post at Gacko, south-east of Mostar, spring 1943.**

SS-Gruppenführer **Artur Phleps.**

Knight's Cross for Artur Phleps

On June 21, 1943, for valor demonstrated as commander of Prinz Eugen, Phleps was promoted to the rank of *SS-Obergruppenführer und General der Waffen-SS* and was awarded the Knight's Cross upon the recommendation of *Reichsführer-SS* Himmler himself, with the following citation[7]: "SS-Obergruppenführer und General der Waffen-SS *Artur Phleps, during the period from January 20 to March 9, 1943, was assigned as Commander of the* SS-Freiwilligen "Prinz Eugen" Division. *In this position he showed himself to be very capable by commanding his units in an energetic and decisive manner. In conducting the attack, which would prove to be decisive , in the area of Petrovac towards Grahovo, during the period from February 23-28, 1943, it was only the personality of the division commander that was able to lead the division to overcome the mountainous terrain with snow that was a meter and a* half deep and full of woods with crevasses, and to overcome many roadblocks along the Petrovac-Drvar road. The attack was made along a broad front and took a four-brigade enemy force by surprise, which as the operation continued, lost its will to fight and its ability to offer any serious resistance. It was due to the personal strength of will of SS-Obergruppenführer Phleps that the division was able to reach Livno, and later the western side of Mostar. Enemy losses amounted to 1,930 dead by count and a further 1,673 estimated dead, 2,378 wounded, a great haul of captured heavy and light machine guns, as well as a large number of horses and vehicles.

A *Prinz Eugen* Flak battery.

SS-Gebirgsjäger.

SS-Gruppenführer Artur Phleps.

As the situation unfolded in this area, on May 15, 1943, the SS-Freiwilligen Division "Prinz Eugen" pushed forward past the Mostar and Capljina area to the southeast, maintaining the advance and forcing the enemy to carry out an orderly withdrawal past Tschetnik, thus being able to achieve the reunification of a part of the territory that was judged to be impossible. In a short time, the advance of the Division in a southeasterly direction enabled all of the mountainous territory in the areas of Niksic and Gornje-Polje, which was lacking in water and with scarce vegetation, to be occupied. The Division Commander, on his own initiative, allowed these poor areas to be taken. With this, the Division found itself in a favorable position to surround the enemy who was forced to withdraw from the Durmitor massif.

The advance of the Division in the direction of Savnik was slowed down for three days by *tenacious enemy resistance and it was only after a well-executed raid that it was possible to penetrate 400 meters in three places inside Savnik. Another advance in the same direction allowed Zabljak to be liberated. With the cooperation of the 1.Geb.-Div. coming from the east, an enemy escape route to the southeast was blocked. In this tight spot, the enemy bands had gathered large forces on the left flank of the Division, in the area of the Piva, north of the Drina and of the Sutjeska-Bogens road, with the intent of opening an escape route to both the south and the north.*

A *Prinz Eugen* position with a machine gun team armed with a ZB 37 heavy machine gun.

SS-Gebirgsjägers climbing a mountain.

During the night between 30 and 31 May, the Division was ordered to send all available troops to the Savnik area, on the left flank, to prevent the enemy breaking through the front in the area of Mratinje in a southerly direction. It was here that the deciding factor was only the personal energy of SS-Obergruppenführer *Phleps who was able, in the space of two days and two nights, to throw into the fray three battalions, two heavy motorized batteries, two* Flak *platoons and two armored companies that were 180 kilometers away in the Avtovac area. With an overwhelming advance on the 2,000 meter high Maglic massif and passing through the extensive areas north of Cemerno-Smedlo, the Division was able to complete the encirclement, in cooperation with the 118.Infanterie-Division. The physical and fighting qualities shown by the men of SS-*

Freiw.Div. "Prinz Eugen" *on this wild mountainous massif full of gorges, without roads, under snow, rain and fog, were the crowning achievement of all that had until then been accomplished by the* SS-Gebirgs-Division "Prinz Eugen", *which was made up mainly of people from the flatlands. The rapid pace of the operation begun from the Narenta and carried out to the Piva, then the shifting of the tactical focal point of the action and the difficult movement to the right of the Division's left flank that enabled the operation on the Maglic massif to continue, led to the encirclement of the exhausted enemy deployment, and without giving them any respite, allowed them to eliminate all possibility of reaction or resistance by the enemy.*

A *Prinz Eugen* motorcycle unit on the move.

***SS-Gruppenführer* Artur Phleps.**

During this operation SS-Ogruf. Phleps particularly distinguished himself both by his personal courage as well as by his excellent command of the units under his command. The Headquarters has paid honor to SS-Ogruf. Phleps and in a special way to the valor and personal courage shown by his troops in bringing this operation to its conclusion. The strict training methods developed and applied with the highest standards while under his command enabled the Division to behave in an excellent fashion during the ensuing fighting. Considering this extraordinary performance, as Commander of the SS-Frw.-Div. "Prinz Eugen", I ask that SS-Ogruf. Artur Phleps be awarded the Knight's Cross. Signed by the Reichsführer-SS, Heinrich Himmler.

Knight's Cross for SS-Sturmbannführer Dietsche

SS-Stubaf. **Bernhard Dietsche.**

On June 16, 1943, Phleps proposed awarding the Iron Cross to *SS-Stubaf.* Bernhard Dietsche, commander of *II./SS-Geb.Jg.Rgt 2*. The award was officially awarded on 17 July 1943. The citation is as follows[8]: *"As commander, SS-Stubaf. Dietsche had the mission to advance to Niksic on the road outside Plevlja with the motorized detachment of the Division, the II./SSGeb.Jg.Rgt 2, 1.Flak-Zug (anti-aircraft platoon), and a Panzer-Kompanie, and to quickly take possession of Bukovica and of the passages to Savnik. These passages (three road bridges) were spread over a 400-meter arc and cut through the valley, and if they had been blown by the enemy, would have delayed the advance of most of the Division towards Zabljak. The road blocks quickly delayed the advance, so much so that they caused the leading units a laborious advance right from the outset of the operation and kept them busy fighting as far as the southern area of Savnik where, coming from the north, the combat groups led by Schmihuber and Petersen and 8.Kompanie all linked up. On May 29, 1943, SS-Stubaf. Dietsche with 8.Kp. and a Kradschützen-Gruppe (motorcycle group) met up with the Schw.Gr.W. (heavy mortar detachment) and a Pak-Zug (anti-tank platoon) from the battalion, which had just arrived on the scene, with the mission of using its 10cm long guns to support the action in the northern area in front of Krusevice and the suburbs of Mokro. All of this was with the aim of taking control as soon as possible of the switchback roads in the southern part of Savnik that dominated the heights to the southwest. To the east of this area Bachmann's combat group (III./SS-Geb.Jg.Rgt 1) had taken up positions on Hill 1257 (sketch A). The decisive intervention in force and the fire support from the artillery and heavy weapons enabled the 8.Kp., the Kradschützen-Gruppe and SS-Geb.Jg.Rgt 2 to yet rapidly seize the heights in the area to the southwest of Savnik. The Panzer-Kompanie and the Flak-Zug had in the meantime not been able to get past the roadblock in the*

A *Prinz Eugen* **motorcycle unit.**

northern part of Krusevice despite the vigorous use of both of the Divison's engineer companies. I had witnessed how SS-Stubaf. Dietsche with 8.Kp. and the Kradschützen-Gruppe had overcome the road block at Mokro and because of this, I had reminded him of the importance of the capture, with a rapid coup de main, of the road passages at Savnik.

A *Hotchkiss H-39* tank assigned to *Prinz Eugen*.

A *Prinz Eugen* tank in action.

A *Prinz Eugen* forward position, spring 1943.

Knowing this courageous and bold officer, I was aware that he was capable of grasping the reins in a difficult situation. As soon as Dietsche understood the importance of seizing the southwestern heights of Savnik, and to what extent the roadblocks in front of them were slowing the advance, on his own initiative and without awaiting the arrival of the Panzer-Kompanie, *with only the* Kradschützen-Gruppe *and despite the fact that enemy machine gun fire was coming from the hills in front of Savnik, he threw himself forward down towards the bridges, managing to take possession of the first two. The second bridge, which was anchored on its north side to a mountain spur, was reached thirty minutes later (at 12:45) by* 1.Zug *of 8.Kp., that was coming from the hill at Cuklin. Despite the intense fire of the heavy machine guns and mortars, with his weak force Dietsche held onto the mountain spur until 15:00, when the rest of 8.Kompanie came to the rescue. Shortly thereafter the enemy mounted a counterattack which was stopped only because of the personal involvement of this courageous commander. He put up a fierce resistance despite the fact that the right flank of his company was in an unfavorable position and he held on until 16:00 when the appearance of the* Panzer-Kompanie *turned the results of the fighting to our advantage and forced the enemy to withdraw...The depth of preparation, the superior experience and a rare boldness set the tone for this undertaking which took its place in an exemplary manner with all of the previous actions carried out by this exemplary SS commander. Shortly after, with is motorized battalion, he shifted from the right flank of the Division in the Savnik area to the left flank in the area of Avtovac and again decisively returned to the attack. This commander full of initiative once again carried out the orders he was given in an exemplary manner. After having taken up positions in the area to the east of Avtovac, he saw the enemy moving towards Stabna and Jasen.*

From the left: *SS-Ostubaf.* von Gurczy, *SS-Stubaf.* Dietsche, *SS-Staf.* Schmidhuber, *SS-Brigdf.* von Oberkamp and *SS-Gruf.* Artur Phleps.

With the force under his command he headed north in accordance with instructions he had been given and headed to the important passage of Presjeka (2,198 meters) which fell into his hands after a fierce encounter with enemy bands that were pushed back. Not satisfied, on his own initiative, he pushed forward and occupied the Maglic passage (2,386 meters) which dominated the entire area. He reached a position where he was able to see the partisan forces moving to the west in an attempt to break the encirclement on the Sutjeska. With Pak *and machine gun fire and with the support of the long-barrelled 10cm guns, the enemy was forced to wedge himself in the narrow confines of the Cemerno passage and while retreating suffered heavy losses. With the closing of the deployment to the west of the Sutjeska the enormous enemy forces that had been surrounded were destroyed. On this inhospitable and snow-covered mountainous massif far from the supply lines for the columns,* there was Dietsche with his unit anchored like a rock and dominating the most important positons. The sketches provided herewith show the final moves of the operation. In view of all of this, this officer has shown himself worthy to be the first Commander of the SS-Freiwilligen-Gebirgs-Division "Prinz Eugen" to be put forth for the award of the Knight's Cross of the Iron Cross".

An SS motorcycle unit passing through a road block defended by Italian troops, summer 1943.

A *Prinz Eugen* tank on the move, summer 1943.

SS-*Hstuf.* Karl Kaiser.

A brief rest period

A brief rest period followed during which the *Gebirgsjäger* were used as an occupation force in the area around Sarajevo. In early August 1943, the division was transferred along with the *369.Kroatische Infanterie Division* to Herzegovina. The command post was set up in Mostar, along with the artillery regiment, and the *Flak*, signals and engineer detachments. *1.SS-Geb.Jg.Rgt.* took up quarters in the Ljubushki area, and 2. at Bileca and the *Panzerjäger-Bataillon* at Nevesinje. Fighting resumed throughout all of Herzegovina for the entire month, first in the north in the area between Prozor and Konjic, and then in the east in the region between Avtovac and Gacko and to the south as fart as Livno. It seemed as though the partisans were everywhere. The Italians had abandoned those areas and had pulled back along the coast. Even the Croats had quit the area, causing the insurrection to grow and leading to an increase in forced recruitment by the communist partisans. Among the units that were most heavily engaged during this period was Kaiser's cavalry squadron, pitted against a rebel formation consisting of about a thousand men led by the partisan chief Vlado Segrt. Intercepted near Stolac, southeast of Mostar, the unit was attacked by

Kaiser's cavalry and forced to withdraw towards Montenegro. The partisans waited for a few days, then turned back, passing through Gacko, to the east of Stolac, but were attacked again by Kaiser's unit near Slivovica and beaten once again. The partisans suffered the loss of several hundred men between dead and wounded, while Kaiser had 16 dead and 19 wounded.

German soldiers inspecting houses in a Bosnian village, summer 1943.

At the same time the partisan X Brigade of Herzdegovina, with a strength of about 1,500 men, crossed the Narenta near Kalinovik, but was attacked by *II./SS-Geb.Jg.Rgt 2* under Dietsche which engaged the partisans in heavy fighting. On September 1, 1943, the cavalry squadron commanded by *SS-Hstuf.* Kaiser, supported by a motorcycle rifle platoon and by the III Group of the artillery regiment, beat back a new attempt to break through by the rebel group led by Vlado Segrt, almost completely wiping it out, following a series of fierce firefights.

Notes
(1) Heinrich Petersen wasborn on March 31, 1904, at Sonderburg, SS Number 134 299. He had served previously in the *SS-Totenkopf-Division*, first commanding II./T.I.R.3 and later I./T.I.R. 3.
(2) Herbert Vollmer was born on October 29, 1913, SS Number 139 159.
(3) Franz-Josef Krombholz was born on August 13, 1920, at Horni Police (*Oberpolitz* in German) in the current Czech Republic, SS Number 452 003. He served in the *Westland* Regiment of the *Wiking* Division, receiving the Iron Cross Second Class in July 1941 and the First Class in November of the same year.
(4) Horst Strathmann, born on May 17, 1899, at Bad Essen, SS Number 25 885.
(5) Rudolf Bachmann, born on November 7, 1919, at Mannheim, SS Number 46 374.
(6) Karl Ferdinand Reichsritter von Oberkamp, born in Munich on October 30, 1893, SS Number 310 306. He had previously commanded II./LSSAH and III./Deutschland and the *"Germania"* Regiment of *Wiking*.
(7) *Personalakte Artur Phleps*, Berlin Document Center.
(8) *Personalakte Bernhard Dietsche*, Berlin Document Center.

Bibliography
M. Afiero, "7.SS-Freiwilligen-Gebirgs-Division Prinz Eugen", Associazione Culturale Ritterkreuz 2010
M. Afiero, "The 7th Waffen-SS Volunteer Gebirgs Div. Prinz Eugen", Schiffer Publishing (U.S.A.)
Roland Kaltenneger, "Die Gebirgstruppe der Waffen SS 1941-1945", Podzun-Pallas
Otto Kumm,"Worwärts Prinz Eugen!", ed. Munin-Verlag
Otto Kumm, "7.SS-Gebirgs-Division Prinz Eugen im bild", Nation Europa Verlag

SS-Haupsturmführer Philipp Theiss
schwere Panzer Kompanie Commander
by Peter Mooney

Philipp Theiss was born on the 22nd of May 1918 and was an early member of the National Socialist organisations. He was certainly a pre-1933 member of the *Hitlerjugend*, possibly as early as 1929. He progressed on through to the *Hitlerjugend*, from the *Deutsches Jungvolk*, when he turned 14 years old, in 1932. He carried the Alte Kampfer Chevron as a result of these early memberships. Between 1934 and 1936, he moved to the R.A.D., performing a mix of administrative tasks, as well as the conventional R.A.D. training.

Philipp in the *Deutsches Jungvolk*, pre-1930.

In the *Hitlerjugend*, proudly wearing his Reichs Party Badge.

Philipp seen in the RAD work tunic.

In his SS N black uniform.

He was a member of the *Abteilung 224.*, serving in the *3.Kompanie* under *Truppenführer* Scholl. During his time with the R.A.D., it appears that he took part in a leadership course. At the start of December, he moved to the *SS-Verfügungstruppe* and was placed with the *SS 'Nurnberg'*, or *SS 'N'*. That formation was initially designated to provide guard duties at the Nuremberg rallies, but that never took place. Instead, that formation was placed under the command of *SS-Deutschland*, at the time commanded by *SS-Standartenführer* Felix Steiner. Throughout 1937, Philipp undertook his training which included a route-march through southern Bavaria, during February. Alternating between the traditional black SS uniform and the newer field-grays, the spring of 1937 put Philipp and his

Kameraden through their paces, with MG training, route-marches, ceremonial activities and then as the summer beckoned, official parade duty. They revolved around Munich, with guard duty at the Honour Temple and the *Feldherrnhalle*.

Philipp and Kameraden during the state visit by Mussolini to Munich in September 1937.

Philipp and Kameraden from *SS-Rgt. Deutschland* visit the heavy cruiser *Deutschland*, 1937.

Official visits from Rudolf Hess in June, followed by Hitler and Mussolini in September, once again seen the men of SS 'N' in their black uniforms. The second half of that year seen them in the field-grays more frequently and the emphasis on fitness is evident from the photos in his surviving collection. Further route-marches, some using bicycles, sports events and trips to the *Kriegsmarine* heavy cruiser *Deutschland*, were amongst some of his activities. One of his identified commanders at that time, was future Knight's Cross holder Herbert Kuhlmann. 1938 would see some notable actions for Philipp, with him obtaining *SS-Sturmmann* rank during that year. In addition, he was part of the formations that took part in the annexations of Austria and also the Sudetenland, under the command of *SS-Deutschland*. Interlaced throughout the years up to this point, is correspondence with Else Dasch. From some of the items in the surviving collection, it is evident that she too was an early supporter of the National Socialist organisations, being a member of the B.D.M. Following the actions in the Sudetenland, Philipp gave her a small wooden jewellery box, inscribed in the inside lid with a commemoration of the Sudetenland action.

Philipp walks close by Feliz Steiner during the Austrian annexation, 1938.

Onboard the rail transports to the Sudetenland region in 1938.

By the end of 1939, he was serving with the *SS-Kradschutzen Ersatz Kompanie* in Ellwangen, staying with them into 1940. He obtained *SS-Unterscharführer* rank around this time. By April of 1940, he had been moved to the *SS-Regiment Der Führer*. He was only with them for a few months, before moving to the SS officer's school at Bad Tölz. He took part in the 5th wartime course, which lasted from the 2nd of September 1940 through to the 10th of April 1941. He progressed through the various officer training ranks in that time, as evidenced through the corresponding documents in his surviving items. Sports were there too and he added the S.A. Sports Badge to his existing awards. Leaving there with *SS-Standartenoberjunker* rank, he quickly obtained *SS-Untersturmführer* rank on the 20th of April 1941.

The Axis Forces

Philipp seen during the 1940-41 winter, as he undertakes his officer training at Bad Tolz.

A formal portrait photo to mark his promotion and addition of the Iron Cross and Black Wound Badge 1941.

His next front line action followed soon after that, with him moving across the Soviet border in July with *SS-Regiment Der Führer*, under Otto Kumm. He added the Second Class Iron Cross on the 28th of that month, with the Black Wound Badge following on the 23rd of August (for a wound back on the 6th of July). That wound may have been significant enough to remove him from the front line, as we know he was in hospital in Bad Kreuznach before the end of 1941 (meaning that he was not eligible for the Russian front Medal, awarded in 1942). It may also be that he suffered a second wound later in the autumn? He remained in hospital into early-1942, then re-joined *Der Führer*, as they were being re-built in France in 1942. Whilst there, the award of the Infantry Assault Badge was approved by Otto Kumm. During that spell in France, Philipp moved to the *SS-Regiment Langemarck*, being placed as a Platoon Leader in their 6. Kompanie. One of his fellow officers then, was future Knight's Cross holder Ernst Tetsch. Whilst with *Langemarck*, he was sent to the *Volkswagen* works to test out the new *Kubelwagen*. Before the end of 1942, Else and Philipp got married. Despite 1942 providing him with many changes and challenges, he was not done yet! In November, *Langemarck* was disbanded and the majority of the staff unit were moved to the *Panzer Regiment* of *Das Reich*, which was nearing the end of its training; for Philipp, that would be a fateful move. It would also appear that he was promoted to *SS-Obersturmführer* in late-1942, possibly the 9th of November. He was placed with their *8. Panzer Kompanie*, who were being trained on the *Tiger* tank. It was with that formation that he went back to the east in early-1943. From the surviving correspondence, it was clear that they were moved at short notice – a terse letter from

Else indicates that to have been the case! He fought in his *Tiger* during Kharkov, although *Das Reich*'s Tigers seen limited action there. The surviving photographs show that he was the II. Platoon commander at that stage, in panzer number '821'. During that phase, Philipp was once again under the command of Herbert Kuhlmann.

Philipp and the men of *SS-Regiment Langemarck*, 1942.

Philipp and Else, January 1943, Fallingbostel.

The period in-between Kharkov and Kursk was a busy one for the *Das Reich* Tiger men. They received additional panzers, which increased their initial strength of 10 that they started 1943 with. He was present during the heavily photographed April 1943 ceremony where his former *Der Führer* commander, Otto Kumm, was informed of the award of the Oakleaves to his existing Knight's Cross. In Philipp's surviving photos, there are images showing him on and around the famous '*Tikki*' Tiger tank. Prior to the start of the Kursk Offensive in July, the *8. Kompanie* were renamed as the *schwere Panzer Kompanie* and their vehicles

The Axis Forces

Philipp seen as an *Obersturmfuhrer*, April 1943 within *Das Reich Tiger Kompanie*.

received a corresponding re-numbering; Philipp's tank carried the number S11 for that next battle. The initial phase of the fighting once again seen limited actions for the *Das Reich* Tigers, with the *Leibstandarte* stablemates bearing the brunt further to the east. That changed close to the high point, when on the 11th of July, Philipp was given command of the *Kompanie*. That same day, he had seen the former commander be evacuated, due to wounding, as well as the initial replacement commander being killed! Philipp was ordered forward on the 15th of July, after another few days of inaction. It was on that day that his commander's cupola received a direct hit, just as he stood with his head out; that enemy round instantly decapitated him. News was sent to Else, via Albin von Reitzenstein, which began a very challenging period for her. Having to pick up the pieces and survive financially, she begun a series of letters to determine what her life looked like after the loss of her husband. Philipp received the posthumous award of the First Class Iron Cross and also promotion to *SS-Hauptsturmführer* (backdated to the 1st of July 1943). The final wartime document we have, from the surviving items of Philipp / Else, is a travel permit in late-1944, allowing her train travel to visit his parents; Else survived the war, but we have no date of death for her. The life of Philipp and Else is covered in the brand new publication from *Loyalty and Honour Publishing*, 'Das Reich Tiger Commander', released at the end of January and available to add to your library. Visit www.lahpublishing.com for details and contact to order. I am grateful to the owner of Philipp Theiss' surviving archive, Andy McNicol, who allowed me access to that extensive material, from which the book was made possible. The research in tying all of the elements together, to paint a comprehensive insight into this former *SS-Panzerman* was undertaken by myself.

Hitler's Cossacks
by Sergio Volpe

Cossack horsemen enlisted in the German army (*Signal*).

Major Kononov with his *Adjutant*, in German uniform.

The first Cossack communities appeared in the Ukrainian steppe in the mid-15th century. Different and contradictory theories have been put forward on the ethnic and historical origin of these communities, often dictated by propaganda and ideology. This uncertainty is mainly due to the lack of historical documents to the fact that the term '*Cossack*' has often been used to define a lifestyle rather than an ethnic group. The same etymology of the term has given rise to different interpretations leading to false conclusions. According to some historians, the Cossacks descend from the nomadic peoples of Turkish origin who gradually became enslaved. According to others, they are fugitives of different origins sheltered in the steppe, to escape the domination of Moscow and the Poles. Rosenberg even found Germanic descent for them. Depending on where they settled, the Cossack communities of Terek, Don and Volga were created. The czars enlisted them in armed communities and engaged them in defending the borders of their empire. During the Russian civil war, after the Bolshevik revolution of 1917, most of the Cossacks sided with the White armies and when they were defeated, they were persecuted by Stalin, deprived of their lands and their freedom.

In the service of the Reich

Oberstleutnant **Kononov.**

General Piotr Krasnov.

The first Cossack chief to join the German army was *Major* Ivan Nikititch Kononov. Born on April 2, 1900, Kononov was the son of a Don Cossack captain, originally from the *Stanitsa* (village) of Novoniko-Laevsk, executed with his bride by the Communists in 1918. To hide his bourgeois origins and escape repression, the young Kononov enlisted in the Red Army in 1920, then joined the *Komsomol* (Communist youth) in 1924. A simple soldier, he served in the 14th Cossack Division of Budienny's 1st Cavalry Army, before becoming an officer in 1922. In 1927 he joined the Communist Party and attended the course at the Moscow Military Academy. Until 1935, he held various commands within the 5th Cavalry Division *'Blinov'*, until he became regimental commander. Admitted to the Frunze Military Academy in Moscow, he graduated with the status of general staff officer. He distinguished himself during the Finnish campaign, in command of the 436th Motorized Rifle Regiment of the 155th Motorized Rifle Division and this earned him the award of the order of the Red Star. In June 1941, when the Germans invaded Russia, he was still in command of the 436th Rifle Regiment. Apparently, Kononov was the archetype of the Red Army officer, but in reality he detested the Soviet regime and waited for the right moment to turn against it. On August 3, 1941, the 436th Rifle Regiment was engaged in the Mogilev region to face *Panzergruppe 3*. Kononov organized a daring counterattack which was about to succeed, when after informing his officers, he decided to send an emissary to the German lines. He brought a message to the Germans in which Kononov expressed his willingness to move on their side, to lay the foundations for the formation of a nucleus of a future *'Russian liberation army'*. The emissary returned with a positive response. At that point, Kononov summoned his men and gave the following speech: "... *My victorious soldiers, I decided to speak to you from the bottom of my heart: I chose this day to declare war on Stalin and the communist regime. I consequently have the intention to cross the front line with those who want it. Those who want to join me to fight for our Mother Russia, put themselves on my right, those who want to stay on my left* ".

Charge of a Cossack unit in the service of the Germans on the Eastern Front.

Cossacks swear allegiance to Hitler.

A few hours later, the entire regiment showed up in front of the German lines. Despite Hitler's orders, which had forbidden the Germans to deal with and arm the Russian deserters, General von Schenkendorf, commander of the German forces in the rear of the Center Armies Group, authorized Kononov to form a Cossack regiment which was assigned the number 102. This unit, the first of its kind, was used by German commands against the partisan gangs that infested the rear of the *Heeresgruppe Mitte*. Kononov's example did not go unnoticed among the thousands of Cossack emigrants. On December 20, 1941, the Cossack general Piotr Nikolaievitch Krasnov, old ataman of the Cossacks of the Don and hero of the civil war, who took refuge in Berlin, sent the following letter to Kononov: "... *Dear Ivan Nikitovich, accept by me and by that of all the old Cossack officers, my most sincere congratulations. We look with great interest on your courageous choice in the fight against communism. Our territories of the Don, Kuban, Terek and the Urals await their release and for them, as for us, you are our only hope. We want to assure you that we are all with you and we wish you good health and many successes ".*

Some photos taken by the SS-PK Mobius in the summer of 1942, in the operating sector of the SS *Wiking* division, showing old Caucasian Cossacks, dressed in their typical elements: the *cherkeska* or *chokha* (the traditional tunic), the *Kubanka* (the typical Astrakhan headdress) and the Caucasian dagger, the *Kindjal*. On the chest, there are the characteristic 'cartridge cases', called *gazyrnitsy*, once intended to holding individual cartridges.

Caucasian Cossacks, Summer 1942.

At the beginning of 1942, an order from Hitler decreed that the units made up of Russian volunteers (*Osttruppen*), should not exceed the strength of a battalion and that they should be integrated into German units. Kononov's regiment was meanwhile renamed as *Kosaken-Abteilung 600*. Thanks to the intervention of General von Schenkendorf, he retained his staff and his Cossack officer cadres. As for Kononov, because of the successes achieved by his unit, he was promoted to the rank of *Oberstleutnant* in the autumn of 1942. In the summer of 1942, the enlistment of the Cossacks took place. At that time, the 1st Panzer Armee of *Generaloberst* von Kleist was advancing in the Cossack territories. As soon as they arrived in the territories of Don, Kuban and Terek, numerous Cossacks spontaneously presented themselves to the German units offering their services. Among them, also the old hero of the Terek Cossacks, Colonel Nikolai Kulakov. Severely injured in 1918, Kulakov lost both his legs and remained hidden in a cave in his native village making himself believed dead.

Caucasian volunteers from Terek or Kuban, September 1942.

A Cossack horseman in the service of the Germans in the Caucasus, with the *cherkeska* and the *Kubanka*, October 1942.

His reappearance raised the enthusiasm of all the Terek Cossacks. With these new volunteers, Cossack units were organized which went to support the armored divisions to carry out reconnaissance. During its advance, the *LX.Pz.Korps* used a squadron of Cossacks from the Don and the Kuban to secure and guard numerous captured Soviet soldiers[1]. Other Cossacks were engaged as escort for troops in the rear. Some sotnie[2], fully equipped and on horseback, made themselves available to the German security divisions to ensure the protection of the rear.

The Cossack district of the Kuban

In October 1942, the Germans settled in Kuban, a semi-autonomous Cossack district, with a population of about 160,000 people. In addition, a Cossack national party was created led by Vassili Glazkov, who recognized Hitler as the defender of the Cossack nation. In the same period, the Cossacks of the Don, taking advantage of the destruction of the Soviet administrative structure, revived their old traditions.

Cossack volunteer in German service.

Cossacks horsemen in German service, 1942.

They elected an ataman (Cossack leader) in the person of Sergei Vassilievitch Pavlov[3]. Shortly after his election as an *Ataman*, Pavlov created a first regiment of the Don Cossacks in August 1942. This regiment, completely independent of the Germans and in the exclusive service of the Cossacks, was equipped with light weapons stolen from the Soviets. Pavlov's forces increased to the point of including a dozen regiments and numerous sotnias. The Germans delegated a liaison officer, *Hauptmann* Müller, to the *Ataman* Pavlov. The latter allowed Pavlov to access the weapons and equipment depots captured in the departments of the fleeing Red Army.

However, the formation of all these Cossack units was not slow in attracting the attention of the German High Command.

Since 1942, an officer of the OKH, the *Oberst* von Freytag-Loringhoven, obtained authorization to form Cossack units under German control. To do this, he set up a recruiting center in an old ammunition factory located in Voenstroy-Seleschina. This initiative was crowned with success and real Cossack units led by German officers were immediately created. These units were formed with the Cossacks 'liberated' by German forces during their advance in the Caucasus, but also with prisoners of war or Cossack deserters[4].

Cossack units

At the end of 1942, the main Cossack units in the *Wehrmacht* were:

Cossack horsemen in the German army, October 1942.

- The *Kosaken Abteilung 600*, under the orders of the *Major* Ivan Kononov, comprising about 1,700 men and 77 officers (60% were Cossacks).

- The *Jungschulz, Lehmann* and *von Wolff* regiments, named after the three *Oberstleutnants* of the Southern and Central Armies Group, who formed these Cossack units, each comprising about 2,000 men, led by 160 German officers and non-commissioned officers. The *Jungschulz* regiment was successfully engaged in protecting the flank of German forces in the Mozdok-Edisya-Atchikulak sector.

- The *Kosaken-Reiter-Regiment 'Platov'* (named after the famous leader of the Napoleonic period), created in 1942.

- The *Reiterverband Boeselager*, a horse unit comprising about 650 Cossacks engaged as a security force in the rear of the Army Group Center.

- The *Kosaken Regiment 6* (or *Plastun Regiment*, infantry regiment): an infantry unit created by *Major* von Renteln, a German-Baltic, an old officer of the Czarist army horse guard. This unit, comprising two battalions (622 and 623) and an independent company (638), would later become the *Grenadier-Regiment 360*.

(To be continued)

Notes

[1] This small unit, led by Captain Zagorodnyi, was later trained and transformed into a Cossack squadron identified as 1./82, employed on the Eastern front until May 1944. This squadron was transferred to the western front, in the region of Saint-Lô, where it was completely annihilated.

[2] Sotnia is a military term of Slavic origin. The term refers to one hundred and can be considered an equivalent of about one company.

[3] Born in Novocherkassk, capital of the Don Cossacks, in 1896, after a passage to the Don cadet school and then to Nikolaevsky cavalry school, he became second lieutenant in 1914. His brilliant conduct at the front earned him the grant of the Cross of St.George. At the outbreak of the civil war, he fought against the Bolsheviks. After the war, he returned to his home region. Fitted with false documents, he managed to get a job as an engineer in an automobile factory.

[4] In 1941, in the Red Army, there were about 100,000 soldiers of Cossack origin.

Bibliography
Massimiliano Afiero, "*I volontari stranieri di Hitler*", Ritter edizioni
Francois de Lannoy, "*Les cosacques de Pannwitz*", Editions Heimdal
D. Littlejohn, "*Foreign Legion of the Third Reich, Vol. 4*", R. Bender Publishing
Erich Kern, "*I Cosacchi di Hitler*", Ritter edizioni

The SS Generals Walter and Friedrich-Wilhelm Krüger
Many Similarities, Many Differences – Part 2
by Michael D. Miller
with translation assistance from Gary Costello

Friedrich-Wilhelm Krüger
SS-Obergruppenführer und General der Waffen-SS und Polizei

SS-Obergruppenführer Friedrich-Wilhelm Krüger (*Bayerische Staatsbibliothek*).

Formal portraits of Friedrich-Wilhelm Krüger in civilian attire during the late 1920s.

Born: 08.05.1894 in Straßburg/Elsaß.

Suicide: 10.05.1945 at a U.S. Army prisoner of war assembly area in Gundertshausen / Kreis Eggelsberg/Oberösterreich.

NSDAP-Nr.: 171 199 (Joined 15.11.1929)
SS-Nr.: 6 123 (Joined 00.08.1930)

Promotions

22.03.1914: *Leutnant* (*ohne Patent*; 16.06.1914: Granted Patent vom 16.06.1914)
00.00.1915: *Oberleutnant*
00.08.1930: *SS-Anwärter*
01.02.1931: *SS-Mann*
16.03.1931: *SS-Sturmführer*
03.04.1931: *SA-Sturmführer*
31.07.1931: *SA-Oberführer*
10.09.1931: *SA-Gruppenführer*
27.06.1933: *SA-Obergruppenführer*
25.01.1935: *SS-Untersturmführer*
25.01.1935: *SS-Obergruppenführer*
08.04.1941: *General der Polizei*
07.05.1942-09.11.1943: *Staatssekretär* (*Generalgouvernement*)
08.07.1944: Authorized to wear the insignia of a *General der Waffen-SS* (*mit Wirkung vom 20.05.1944*)

Career

00.00.1900-00.00.1903: Attended *Bürgerschule* in Rastatt

00.00.1904-00.00.1909: Attended the humanistic Gymnasium in Rastatt

00.00.1909-00.03.1914: Attended the *Kadettenhaus* in Karlsruhe and the *Haupt-Kadettenanstalt* Groß-Lichterfelde (did not graduate).

22.03.1914-11.11.1918: Entered military service, assigned to *Kgl. Preußische Infanterie-Regiment "von Lützow" (1. Rheinische) Nr. 25* (Aachen). From 04.08.1914-11.11.1918, he was assigned successively as a *Zugführer* in, then *Führer* of, an *MG-Kompanie*; as *Ordonnanzoffizier*; and *Regiments-Adjutant*. He was wounded three times.

His wartime deployments were as follows:

Western Front: 22.08.1914-00.00.1916
Eastern Front: 00.00.1916-00.11.1916
Western Front: 17.11.1916-11.11.1918

The Axis Forces

Freikorp soldier.

00.00.1917-00.00.1917: Half-year detachment from his regiment for assignment as *Ordonnanzoffizier* to the staff of *208.Infanterie-Division*.

00.02.1919-00.07.1919: Service with *Freikorps "II. Marinebrigade, Wilhelmshaven"* of *1. Torpedobootflottille* (known as the *"Eiserne Torpedobootflottille"*)

00.07.1919-00.03.1920: Service with *Freikorps Lützow* in the Ruhrgebiet.

00.05.1920: Discharged from military service.

00.00.1920-00.00.1923: *Prokurist* (authorized representative) of a publishing firm in Berlin.

00.00.1923-00.00.1924: Employed as forwarding clerk in a publishing firm, Berlin.

00.00.1924-00.00.1928: *2.Vorstandsmitglied* (2nd member of the board) and Direktor of *Berliner Müllabfuhr AG*, Berlin.

00.00.1928-00.00.1929: Unemployed.

00.00.1929-00.00.1933: Worked as an independent businessman.

15.11.1929: Joined the NSDAP in Berlin.

00.11.1929-00.00.1932: Served as an organizer of all significant demonstrations and other actions of the NSDAP during this period.

00.08.1930: Applied for membership in the SS.

01.02.1931: SS membership application accepted.

16.03.1931-03.04.1931: Assigned as an *SS-Führerz.b.V.* to the staff of *SS-Abschnitt III* (Berlin) and as *Beauftragter für die SS-Angelegenheiten* (Representative for SS Affairs) in Gau Brandenburg (responsible for the *15. SS-Brigade*)

03.04.1931: Assigned to the SA.

05.04.1931-09.09.1931: *Stabsleiter* of *SA-Gruppe Ost* (Berlin) and *Vertreter des Gruppenführers der SA-Gruppe Ost*.

05.04.1931-09.09.1931: *Führer* of the *SA Gausturm* in Brandenburg (m.d.F.b. until 30.07.1931, then permanent from 31.07.1931).

10.09.1931-13.04.1932: *Führer* of *SA-Gruppe Ost* (*kommissarischer* until 13.10.1931, succeeding Paul Schulz, then permanent from 13.04.1932). SA officially banned by the German government, 13.04.1932-14.06.1932.

16.06.1932-01.03.1933: *Reichsführer* of the *Nationalsozialistische Schülerbund* (NSS, National-Socialist Students' League).

01.07.1932-27.06.1933: *Gruppenführer z.b.V.* and Chef of the *Gruppenstab z.b.V.beim Stab der Obersten SA-Führers* (Berlin).

31.07.1932-12.09.1932: Member of the *Reichstag* (Wahlkreis 5, Frankfurt/Oder).

04.10.1932-01.07.1933: *Vertreter der SA im Reichskuratorium für Jugendertüchtigung* (Representative of the SA to the ReichCommittee for Youth Training).

The "*HJ- und BDM Reichsjugendtag*" in Potsdam, 01.-02.10.1932. From left to right: *SA-Gruppenführer* Friedrich-Wilhelm Krüger, Dr. Goebbels, and *SA-Gruppenführer* Karl Ernst.

SA-Obergruppenführer Krüger in 1934 (NARA).

24.12.1932-01.02.1933: Member of the *Reichstag* (*Wahlkreis 5*, Frankfurt/Oder).

00.02.1933-00.02.1933: Together with Reinhard Heydrich, assigned as a *Polizei- und Sicherheitsexperte* (police and security expert) to the German delegation to the International Disarmament Conference in Geneva, Switzerland.

05.03.1933-14.10.1933: Member of the *Reichstag* (*Wahlkreis 5*, Frankfurt/Oder).

01.04.1933-01.07.1933: *Leiter* of the *Reichskuratorium für Jugendertüchtigung* (Reich Committee for Youth Training).

27.06.1933-26.10.1934: *Chef des Ausbildungswesens* [AW] *der SA* (Chief of the SA Training Services Command).

01.07.1933-09.08.1934: *Führer der SA-Grenzeinheiten* (Leader of SA Border Units).

18.07.1933-00.03.1935: *Inspekteur des Seesports der SA* (Inspector of SA Water Sports).

SA-Obergruppenführer Krüger in 1934 (NARA).

00.11.1933-00.01.1935: *Vertreter der Obersten SA-Führung im Reichsverteidigungsrat* (Representative of the Supreme SA Leadership to the Reich Defense Council).

12.11.1933-08.05.1945: Member of the *Reichstag* (*Wahlkreis 5*, Frankfurt/Oder).

05.12.1933: At a conference of SA leaders in Feldafing, *SA-Stabschef* Röhm announced that henceforth, the *AW-Schulen* (schools of Krüger's SA Training Services Command) would be subordinated to the leaders of *SA-Obergruppen* and -*Gruppen*.

28.02.1934: In agreement with *Generalmajor* Walther von Reichenau, head of the *Ministeramt in the Reichswehrministerium*, ordered that the SA would be utilized for border protection duties under the commanders of *Wehrkreise* (defense districts) and *Grenzabschnitte* (border sectors). With great reluctance, the *Reichswehr* introduced special training courses for SA officers on matters of border defense.

SA-Obergruppenführer Krüger attends an official function early in 1934. From left to right: Josef Dietrich, Paul Körner, Krüger, Julius Schaub, Dr. Goebbels, Wilhelm Brückner (in SA uniform), Ernst Röhm, Hitler, Werner von Blomberg, Karl Ernst, and Georg von Detten.

Berlin, 20.07.1934: *SA-Obergruppenführer* Krüger during the swearing-in ceremony for members of the Berlin Stadtrat. To either side of him are the deputy Gauleiter of Berlin, Artur Görlitzer (left) and *SA-Oberführer* Achim von Arnim (right).

SA-Obergruppenführer Krüger poses with senior leaders of the SS, Police, and *Luftwaffe* in the late summer or early fall of 1934. From right to left: Krüger, Reinhard Heydrich, Erhard Milch, unknown, Himmler, Karl Wolff, and Kurt Daluege.

20.07.1934-06.11.1935: *Ratsherr der Reichshauptstadt Berlin* (city counselor of the Reich Capital, Berlin).

00.00.1934-00.00.19__: *Preußischer Staatsrat.*

26.10.1934: Separated from the SA. Prior to the purge of the SA on 30.06.1934, he had acted as an informer against Röhm and other SA leaders, thus incurring the lasting hatred of his former colleagues.

26.10.1934-06.03.1935: *Chef des Ausbildungswesens* (Chef AW).

25.01.1935: Reentered SS service. His staff as Chef AW was placed under SS control.

25.01.1935-01.03.1936: Assigned to the staff of the *Reichsführer-SS.*

01.07.1935-01.08.1935: Attached to *SS-Oberabschnitt Mitte* (Dresden).

01.03.1936-16.05.1938: *Inspekteur der "Grenz- und Wacheinheiten" (Allgemeine-SS)* in the SS-Hauptamt.

08.11.1936: Sworn in by the *Reichsführer-SS* at Dachau as a *Hüter des Bluts- und Lebensgesetzes der Schutzstaffel* (Guardian of the Blood and Life Statute of the SS).

26.01.1937-16.05.1938: *Schiedmann der große Schiedhof beim Reichsführer-SS* (arbitrator the arbitration court for matters concerning officers in the rank of *SS-Obersturmbannführer* and above).

20.07.1937: Appointed as an honorary member of the *Volksgerichtshof* (five-year appointment).

16.05.1938-09.10.1939: *Inspekteur der gesamten SS-Reiterei* (Inspector of all mounted units of the SS), under the *Chef* of the *SS-Hauptamt.*

Formal portraits of Friedrich-Wilhelm Krüger as an *SS-Obergruppenführer* (NARA).

00.01.1939: Appointed as *Leiter* of the *Obersten Behörde des Deutschen Reitsports* (Supreme Authority for German Equestrian Sports).

04.10.1939-09.10.1939: *Höherer SS- und Polizeiführer beim Verwaltungschef des Militärbefehlshabers Lodsch* (Higher SS and Police Leader to the Administration Chief of the Military Commander in Łódź), Poland.

04.10.1939-09.11.1943: *Höheren SS- und Polizeiführers beim Oberverwaltungschef* [Dr. Hans Frank] *für den Bereich des Oberbefehlshabers Ost (m.d.W.d.G.b.)*. He assumed the duties of this post on 09.10.1939. On 26.10.1939, it was redesignated *Höherer SS- und Polizeiführer beim Generalgouverneur für die besetzten polnischen Gebiete in Krakau* ("*Höherer SS- und Polizeiführer Ost*"; Short title: HSSPF Ost) (Kraków). In this capacity, he also served as *Gerichtsherr of SS- und Polizeigericht VII (Kraków)*. Succeeded by Wilhelm Koppe. Under his authority as HSSPF were the *Befehlshaber der Ordnungspolizei* [BdO] *im Generalgouvernement* as well as the following *SS- und Polizeiführer (SSPF)* commands: Krakau, Lublin, Radom, Warschau, and- from August 1941- Lemberg.

On 18.04.1946, former *Generalgouverneur* **Dr. Frank testified at Nürnberg**: *The relations between him and myself became quite impossible. He wanted a peculiar kind of SS and police regime, and that state of affairs could be solved only in one way-either he or I had to go. I think that at the last moment, by the intervention of Kaltenbrunner, if I remember correctly, and of Bach-Zelewski, this remarkable fellow was removed... Of course it was a struggle for power. I wanted to establish a power in the sense of my*

Friedrich Wilhelm Krüger sits nearest the camera together with *Generalgouverneur* Dr. Frank and Frank's deputy, Josef Bühler in Kraków, ca. 1940 (*Roger Bender*).

memoranda to the Führer, *and therefore I had to fight the power of violence, and here personal viewpoints separated altogether.* (Trial of the Major War Criminals Before the International Military Tribunal, Nuremberg, Volume XII).

Frank's official diary contains the following statements he made to Krüger at a meeting of his staff on 25.01.1943: Staatssekretär *Krüger, you know that orders of the* Reichsführer-SS *can be carried out by you only after you have spoken with me. This was omitted in this instance. I express my regret that you have carried out an order from the* Reichsführer *without first informing me, in accordance with the orders of the* Führer. *According to that order, instructions of the* Reichsführer-SS *may be carried out here in the* Generalgouvernement *only after I have previously given my approval. I hope that this is the last time that that is overlooked; because I do not want to trouble the* Führer *about every single case of this kind. It is not possible for us to disregard* Führer *orders, and it is out of the question that in the sphere of police and security direct orders from the* Reichsführer *should be carried out over the head of the man who has been appointed here by the* Führer; *otherwise I should be completely superfluous.* (Excerpt from Document 2233-PS, in ibid).

On a number of occasions, Dr. Frank complained of Krüger's actions to *Reichsminister* **Dr. Lammers of the** *Reichskanzlei***. The following is excerpted from Lammer's testimony before the IMT Nürnberg on 08.04.1946:** *On this point he addressed repeated complaints to me, so that I might take them to the* Führer, *which, however, I could do only in part. In one point, however, we did want to help him. In the Government General there had been established a Secretariat of State for the security system. This was under Krüger, then Higher SS and Police Chief. This, however, functioned for only 4 to 6 weeks and then differences of opinion in this field broke out once more. The State Secretary for Security, Krüger, stated, "I receive my orders from Himmler." If the Governor General complained about that, then Himmler said, "These are all unimportant matters. I certainly must be able to rule on them directly." The Governor General said, "But for me they are not unimportant; even those things are important to me". The channels of command and the co-operation with the Governor General were not being observed, and it is therefore perfectly understandable that Herr Frank had a very difficult position with respect to the police system. [...] He repeatedly offered his resignation, because of these sharp conflicts which he had, with Himmler in particular, and because Hitler usually decided that he was in the wrong and Himmler in the right. Many statements of his* *intention or desire to resign were brought to me, some of which I was not even allowed to submit to the Führer. But I informed the Führer of the Governor General's intentions of resigning and the Führer several times refused Frank's offer to resign. [...] Reichsführer Himmler personally was indubitably an opponent of Frank's. There is cause for me to assume from various disapproving statements made by Himmler with regard to Frank that Himmler would have liked it very much if Frank had been removed from his position; and Reichsleiter Bormann who also was not very well disposed to Frank's personality, would have liked it also. (ibid).*

Kraków, 01.09.1940. German officials celebrate the first anniversary of the invasion of Poland. Left to right: Richard Schalk, Friedrich-Wilhelm Krüger, *SA-Brigadeführer* Dr. Karl Strölin (head of the *Deutschen Auslandsinstitut in Stuttgart*), *SA-Obergruppenführer* Ludwig Siebert (*Ministerpräsident* of Bayern), *Generalgouverneur* Dr. Frank, and *SS-Brigadeführer* Dr. Otto Gustav Wächter (Gouverneur of Distrikt Krakau). (*Polish Digital Archives*).

On 23.04.1946, Frank's Staatssekretär and deputy, Dr. Josef Bühler, testified at Nürnberg regarding the difficulties between the Generalgouvernement authorities and the obstreperous HSSPF Krüger:

The relationship with the Police under Krüger had always been hostile, and whenever the administration department had 'any wish that involved police jurisdiction, such wishes had always been frustrated by Krüger; therefore, after Krüger had left Krakow I tried to establish a comradely relationship with the new Higher SS and Police Leader, so that in this manner I could influence the work of the Police and the methods employed by them.

(Trial of the Major War Criminals Before the International Military Tribunal, Nuremberg, Volume XII).

09.10.1939-26.10.1939: *Höherer SS- und Polizeiführer im Bereich des Grenzabschnitts Mitte (Militärbezirk Lodsch)*.

30.10.1939-22.10.1943: *Beauftragter des RKF im Bereich Krakau* (redesignated *Beauftragter des RKF im Generalgouvernement*, 19.12.1939). In a letter to Ulrich Greifelt dated 25.11.1941, Krüger wrote: "*All racial-political activity in the Generalgouvernement will be coordinated and directed by me and by me exclusively as deputy of the Reichsführer-SS in his capacity as RKFDV*".

08.11.1939: Participated in a conference in Posen with Generalgouverneur Dr. Frank, Wilhelm Koppe (HSSPF in Posen), and Bruno Streckenbach (BdS in Kraków). The main topic discussed was preparations for the deportation of Poles and Jews from the provinces of Danzig-Westpreußen, Posen, and Ostpreußen to the Generalgouvernement.

Kraków, October 1940: Dr. Hans Frank (far left) and an assortment of German officials celebrate the first anniversary of the Generalgouvernement's establishment. A helmeted Friedrich-Wilhelm Krüger stands in the right foreground (*Polish Digital Archives*).

15.12.1939: The *SS-Totenkopf-Reiterstandarte* under *SS-Standartenführer* Hermann Fegelein placed at Krüger's disposal.

14.01.1940: Survived an assassination attempt.

30.01.1940: Participated in a conference in Berlin, chaired by Reinhard Heydrich, concerning "*Evacuation of Poles and Jews from the Warthegau*".

00.04.1940: Honorary member of the *Institut für deutsche Ostarbeit* in Kraków.

00.05.1940: Charged by Generalgouverneur Dr. Frank with carrying out the *außerordentliche Befriedungsaktion* (extraordinary pacification action, code-named "*AB-Aktion*"), approved by Frank on 16.05.1940 and aimed at potential leaders and agents of resistance to Nazi occupation. The "*AB-Aktion*" resulted in the mass arrest of approximately 3,500 "*activists*" (members of the Polish intelligentsia and leadership classes- the nobility, judges, university professors, priests, writers, teachers, politicians, etc.- seen as potential resistance agents) and some 3,000 suspected criminals. These people were massacred by Krüger's SS and Police forces in the forest of Palmiry near Warsaw and other isolated locations throughout the Generalgouvernement.

02.09.1941: Meeting with *Reichsführer-SS* on the topic *"Jewish Question – resettlement out of the Reich."* (*Der Dienstkalender Heinrich Himmlers 1941/42*)

Left: Kraków, April 1941. A heavily retouched photo of Krüger being congratulated by Dr. Frank. In the background are Dr. Eberhard Schöngarth and Julius Riege, Krüger's subordinates in command of the *Sicherheitspolizei/SD* and *Ordnungspolizei*, respectively, in the *Generalgouvernement*. **Right**: Wawel Castle, Kraków, 19.05.1942. Dr. Frank appoints Krüger as State Secretary for Security Affairs in the *Generalgouvernement* administration (*Polish Archives*).

13.10.1941: Meeting with Himmler and Globocnik (lasting two hours, per Himmler's Dienstkalender) aboard the Reichsführer's personal train (*Sonderzug "Heinrich"*) at *Führer* HQ *"Wolfsschanze"* in Rastenburg/Ostpreußen.

28.11.1941: Attended a meeting with Himmler and Heydrich in Berlin, during which they discussed the establishment of a *"zentralen Bearbeitung der Judenangelegenheiten im Generalgouvernement"* (Central Authority for Jewish Matters in the Generalgouvernement). (*Der Dienstkalender Heinrich Himmlers 1941/42*)

20.01.1942: Although he did not personally attend the *"Wannsee Conference"* chaired by Reinhard Heydrich in Berlin, Krüger was represented there by his subordinate, *SS-Oberf.*

The Axis Forces

Friedrich-Wilhelm Krüger with *SS-Brigadeführer und Generalmajor der Polizei* Theobald Thier (right) in 1943. Thier was *SS- und Polizeiführer* for Distrikt Lemberg (29.07.1943-25.02.1944) and was executed in Kraków on 12.07.1949 (Marc Rikmenspoel).

Dr. Eberhard Schöngarth (*Befehlshaber der Sicherheitspolizei und des Sicherheitsdienstes in Krakau*).

14.03.1942: Meeting with Himmler and *SS-Oberführer* Dr. Schöngarth in Kraków.

07.05.1942-09.11.1943: *Staatssekretär für das Sicherheitswesen in der Regierung des Generalgouvernements* (ceremonially appointed to this post by Generalgouverneur Dr. Frank on 19.05.1942).

09.06.1942: Attended the state funeral of Reinhard Heydrich in the *Mosaiksaal* of the *Reichskanzlei*, Berlin.

09.07.1942: Participated in a conference at Friedrichsruh convened by Himmler and also attended by Erich von dem Bach, Hans-Adolf Prützmann, Odilo Globocnik, Kurt Daluege, Bruno Jedicke, Dr. Eberhard Schöngarth, Bruno Streckenbach, Carl Zenner, and Kurt Knoblauch. Topics discussed included the centralization of and the need to pursue a "*hard and ruthless*" war against partisans and the need to reinforce the forces allocated to anti-partisan operations; "*Einsatz Reinhard*" (the extermination of Jews in the Generalgouvernement); and the necessity of creating an army of slave labors for the implementation of *Generalplan Ost* (Himmler's plan for German settlement of the East).

09.07.1942: Charged by Generalgouverneur Dr. Frank "*with the implementation of crop-raising, as well as the labor input of non-German workers in the Generalgouvernement*" and "*with the allocation of labor from non-German laborers for the Reich*" (i.e., rounding them up and sending them to Germany for slave labor).

19.07.1942: Attended a conference in Lublin with Himmler, Odilo Globocnik, Oswald Pohl, and Walter Schellenberg. On the same day, Himmler issued the following order to Krüger:

I herewith order that the resettlement of the entire Jewish population of the Generalgouvernement be carried out and completed by 31. December 1942.

From 31. December 1942, no persons of Jewish origin may remain within the Generalgouvernement, unless they are in the collection camps in Warsaw, Krakow, Czestochowa, Radom, and Lublin. All other work on which Jewish labor is employed must be finished by that date, or, in the event that this is not possible, it must be transferred to one of the collection camps.

These measures are required with a view to the necessary ethnic division of races and peoples for the New Order in Europe, and also in the interests of the security and cleanliness of the German

Reich and its sphere of interest. Every breach of this regulation spells a danger to quiet and order in the entire German sphere of interest, a point of application for the resistance movement and a source of moral and physical pestilence.

For all these reasons a total cleansing is necessary and therefore it will be carried out. Cases in which the date set cannot be observed will be reported to me in time, so that I can see to corrective action at an early date. All requests by other offices for changes or permits for exceptions to be made must be presented to me personally. (IMT Nürnberg Document NO-5574).

Between March 1942 and November 1943, in the *Vernichtungslagern* (extermination camps) of Bełżec, Sobibór, and Treblinka, as well as KL-Lublin (aka Majdanek)- all located in Distrikt Lublin, where Odilo Globocnik was *SS- und Polizeiführer* and director of the operation- some 2,000,000 Jews were exterminated in what was to be code-named "*Einsatz Reinhard*" (aka "*Aktion Reinhard*"). Krüger was fully informed and complicit in the operation. The following passage discusses the euphemistic but revealing language he used in official correspondence regarding officers directly involved in the killing actions:

In June 1942, *SS-Obergruppenführer* Krüger wrote to request that [*SS-Obersturmführer*] Helmuth Pohl, a member of SSPF Lublin and part of [*SS-Sturmbannführer* Hermann] Höfle's deportation staff, be promoted to an officer of the *Waffen-SS* as he was engaged "*with important tasks in the 'Jewish Resettlement' desk*" (im Referat "*Judenumsiedlung*"). Inverted commas were used in the original (HSSPF Ost, "Ernennung zu Führern der Waffen-SS, 8.6.1942, signed Krüger, BDC SS-Personalakte Helmuth Pohl). Krüger referred the SS Personnel Office to a communication written on June 3, 1942 about the task "*Jewish Resettlement*" of the *Reichsführer-SS*, the same day that Globocnik presented a "*Jew folder*" (*Judenmappe*) containing his plans for the second phase of *Aktion Reinhard* to Himmler (SSPF Lublin, 33/42 gRs, Lublin, den 3.6.42, signed. Globocnik, BA NS19/1755, p. 2) In September 1943, Krüger wrote to the HSSPF Niederlande, Hanns-Albin Rauter, trying to place Hermann Höfle in a new job after the completion of *Aktion Reinhard*. Stating that Höfle had had to carry out "*special tasks*" (*Sonderaufträge*), Krüger elaborated by explaining that these had above all consisted of the "*Jew Final Solution Question*" (*Judenendlösungsfrage*), a "*purely confidential matter*" (*reine Vertrauenssache*) that was also especially demanding (Krüger to Rauter, 24.9.43, BDC SS-Personalakte Hermann Höfle). (Jonathan Harrison, Roberto Muehlenkamp, et al, *Belzec, Sobibor, Treblinka. Holocaust Denial and Operation Reinhard*, p. 212-213)

15.09.1942-09.11.1943: *Führer* of *SS-Oberabschnitt Ost* (Kraków). Succeeded by Wilhelm Koppe.

25.01.1943: Meeting with Generalgouverneur Dr. Frank and others in Warsaw.

12.03.1943-20.05.1943: Member of the *Aufsichtsrat* of the SS-owned economic enterprise Ostindustrie GmbH ("*Osti*"), Lublin.

20.04.1943: Survived an assassination attempt while enroute to his headquarters in Kraków. At 0950 hours, as his car was crossing the bridge over the Vistula, the Poles Andrzej Lewinski and Tadeuz Battek threw two bombs at his vehicle. The car sustained serious damage, but Krüger was uninjured. On 23.04.1943, Krüger was presented with an armored limousine on the recommendation of *Reichsleiter* Bormann. On 09.05.1943, the British news agency Reuters erroneously reported: "*General Krüger, known for his cruelty in Poland, was brought down by tommy gun bullets in broad daylight and died a few days later.*"

02.05.1943: Visited the Warsaw Ghetto to observe the *"Großaktion"* (the suppression of the Jewish revolt and deportation of its remaining ca. 56,000 residents to the extermination camp at Treblinka). The operation was overseen from 19.04. to 16.05.1943 by his subordinate, Jürgen Stroop, the fanatical *SS- und Polizeiführer Warschau*, who sent daily reports of his progress via telegram to Krüger.

21.06.1943: Attended a conference chaired by the *Reichsführer-SS,* during which Erich von dem Bach was appointed as *Chef der Bandenkampfverbände* and the *Bandenkampfgebiete* (partisan combating regions) were delineated.

27.08.1943: Submitted a request for sick leave to the *Reichsführer-SS*; Himmler authorized him to take 4 days' vacation in Norway.

00.10.1943-04.11.1943: Overall director and organizer of *"Aktion Erntefest"* (Action Harvest Festival). In October, fearing the prospect of more revolts by armed Jews such as those in the Warsaw Ghetto and in the Treblinka and Sobibór extermination camps, Himmler ordered Krüger to carry out the liquidation of all labor camps (administered by Ostindustrie GmbH), and their Jewish laborers, in the Lublin District. These included the camps of Trawniki, Poniatowa, Budzyn, Pulawy, Zamosc, Biala Podlaska, and in Lublin proper, Lindestraße 7 (in Polish, Lipowa Street), Flugplatz-Lager, and Sportplatz. Himmler had first mentioned the possibility of such an action to Krüger as early as late-August. A few days before the operation, which was under the immediate direction of Globocnik's successor as SSPF in Lublin, Jakob Sporrenberg, Jewish workers were directed to dig *"anti-aircraft ditches"*. Numerous SS and Police units then assembled in the area, and on 03.11.1943 they surrounded KL-Lublin and the Trawniki labor camp, to which were brought prisoners from outlying camps. On the first day, between 0600 and 1700 hours, 16,000 to 18,400 Jews were killed by SS and Police gunfire. By the end of the following day, the total killed in Lublin District camps, as well as other camps in Galicia (such as Janowska Street camp in Lemberg), had risen to 42,000.

08.11.1943: Departed from his posts in the Generalgouvernement, having failed in his power struggle with Dr. Frank. On the same day, he left Kraków. He later wrote, in a letter of 06.04.1944 to the chief of the SS-Personalhauptamt, Maximilian von Herff: "...*After losing my honor and reputation due to my clean, four-year battle in the GG, I hope that it will be granted to me to do my duty as a soldier at the front*".

09.11.1943-31.03.1944: Assigned to the *Persönlichen Stab RFSS (Führerreserve)*.

00.11.1943-00.03.1944: Attached for training as a *Divisionsführer* to the 7. *SS-Freiwilligen-Gebirgs-Division "Prinz Eugen"* in Bosnia.

00.03.1944-00.03.1944: *"beauftragt mit der vertretungsweisen Führung* [charged with acting leadership] of 7. *SS-Freiwilligen-Gebirgs-Division "Prinz Eugen"*.

20.05.1944-26.08.1944: *Kommandeur* of 6.*SS-Gebirgs-Division "Nord"* (assumed command in Finland, 14.06.1944). Succeeded Lothar Debes. Succeeded by Karl-Heinrich Brenner.

26.08.1944-15.02.1945: *Kommandierender General* of *V.SS-Gebirgs-Korps* (m.d.F.b. until 01.10.1944, then permanent). The Korps, with headquarters in Mostar, operated in southern Bosnia under the auspices of *Heeresgruppe E* (*Generaloberst* Alexander Löhr).

Krüger succeeded Artur Phleps and was succeeded by Friedrich Jeckeln. As of 01.08.1944, the following divisions were subordinated to the *Korps*:

7.SS-Gebirgs-Division "Prinz Eugen"
369.Infanterie-Division
118.Jäger-Division
13.Waffen-Gebirgs-Division der SS "Handschar" (kroatische Nr. 1) (under the tactical authority of *XXI.Gebirgs-Armee-Korps*)
21. Waffen-Gebirgs-Division der SS "Skanderbeg" (albanische Nr. 1)
Kroatische Jäger-Brigade 1
Kroatische Gebirgs-Brigade 2

SS-Obergruppenführer Krüger with officers of *7. SS-Freiwilligen-Gebirgs-Division "Prinz Eugen"* in 1944. To his immediate right is *SS-Sturmbannführer* Erich Eberhardt.

At the end of 1944, the *Korps* was withdrawn from the Balkans and transferred to the Frankfurt (Oder)/Guben area where it was subordinated to the *9.Armee* under *Heeresgruppe Weichsel*. As of 01.02.1945, it controlled the following divisions:

391.Sicherungs-Division (4,537 men)
32.SS-Frewilligen-Grenadier-Division "30. Januar" (6,703 men)
286.Infanterie-Division (3,950 men)

20.01.1945-20.02.1945: Assigned as an *SS-Führerz. V. to the Persönlichen Stab RFSS*.

20.02.1945-00.04.1945: Placed in *Führerreserve RFSS* and assigned as *z. V. (zur Verwendung,* at disposal) of the *HSSPF Warthe in Ostpreußen.*

00.04.1945-00.05.1945: *General der Ordnungstruppen* and *Kommandeur* of an *Ordnungspolizei Kampfgruppe* subordinated to *Heeresgruppe Süd* (redesignated *Heeresgruppe Ostmark* on 01.05.1945) in Austria.

Published Work

Das Infanterie-Regiment von Lützow (1. Rhein.) Nr 25 im Weltkriege 1914-1918 (coauthor, with Adolf Hüttmann; 1929)

Decorations & Awards

20.09.1944: *Ritterkreuz des Eisernes Kreuzes* as *SS-Obergruppenführer und General der Waffen-SS und Polizei* for command of 6. *SS-Gebirgs-Division "Nord"/20. Gebirgs-Armee*. Award based on the following proposal by *Reichsführer-SS* Himmler:

Brief statement of reasons and opinions by the immediate superior.

On the 23.05.44, *SS-Obergruppenführer, General der Waffen SS und Polizei,* Friedrich-Wilhelm Krüger took over the leadership of the *6.SS-Geb.Division "Nord"*, which was deployed in the Louchi Sector (Karelien), subordinated to the *XVIII.(Geb.)A.K. (20.(Geb.) Armee).*

Enemy intentions:
On the 25.06.1944, the enemy assembled 3 divisions and attacked the northern flank of the division with the intention of, after the loss of his own northernmost bases, to thrust over the land bridge Jeletjosero-Ssennosero and deep into the flank of the Division, taking control of the area around Okunjewa-guba and with this reconnecting with his own road to the south. In a further thrust to the south to reach the Kiestinki crossroads and with this block the only supply route and to cut off the two divisions deployed in the Louchi sector (*6th SS (Geb.) "Nord"* and the divisional group Kräutler) from their supply bases. In the course of this attack there was still the danger that Russian forces to the north of Ssennosero would thrust in an extension

Friedrich Wilhelm Krüger as commander of *6. SS-Gebirgs-Division "Nord"* in 1944.

towards the northern bank of the Pja Lake and take control of that area. (Which was only secured by a Finnish Luftschutzkompanie) With this, a good road, which leads to Kuusamo und the rear Army area, would have fallen into the hands of the enemy. Kuusamo is a hub for the supply of the XVIII Army. At the same time it was to be expected that the enemy would create further attack focal points by carrying out a frontal assault supported by tanks in the area of the SS road and the southern flank of the *SS-Geb. Jag. Rgt. 12 "MG"*.

Course of Fighting:
In a surprise thrust carried out on 27.06.1944 by far superior forces, it was possible for the enemy to recapture both of their own northerly bases. As an immediate reaction, the *SS-Aufkl. Abt (mot) 6* was deployed against the land bridge Kapanez Lake - Ssennosero.

Left to right: *SS-Untersturmführer* **Hans Petter Hoff** (*Schi-Kompanie/"Nord"*), *Divisionskommandeur* **Friedrich-Wilhelm Krüger**, *SS-Sturmbannführer* **Heinz-Hans Küchle** (*1. Generalstabsoffizier [Ia] of "Nord"*), and *SS-Obersturmführer* **Rolf Ugelstad** (*Schi-Jäger-Bataillon "Norge"*).

The Abt. managed to hold off the advancing enemy for long enough and to inflict such heavy losses on him until additional forces could be freed up. The *Jäger Btl.6 (Heer)* was subordinated to the Division by the Gen. Kdo. Without regard for himself, the *Obergruppenführer* managed to advance this over-cautious and unenergetically led group into the area in question to block the isthmus Jeletjesero - Ssennosero. To counteract the second danger, the advance of the enemy to the north of Ssennosero - Pja lake, the *Obergruppenführer* deployed the *SS-Schtz.Btl.(mot) 6* combined with the *Ski Btl. 82 (Heer)*, which had been subordinated by the Gen.Kdo. of the Division and now together formed the "*Kampfgruppe Lapp*", to the area of the village of Ssennosero with the order to block the strait near Blaupunkt 301. At the same time the *Obergruppenführer* prepared the attack against a strengthened enemy in the strait Jeletjesero - Ssennosero by extracting the Jäger Btl. from the front positions which were weakened by this move. Through attacks carried out by 2 Btl. on the 02.06.1944 and 3 Btl. on the 06.06.1944 it was possible to inflict such heavy losses on the numerically far superior enemy force on the isthmus Jeletjesero - Ssennosero that the enemy had to give up his intention of breaking through and instead set up a defense. At the same time the enemy, who appeared to be of the opinion that his intentions in the area of the village of Ssennosero had been ruined by our *Kampfgruppe*, amassed a strong force (1 Schützen Regt.,4 Schi- Btl.), surrounded the *Kampfgruppe* and attempted to destroy it by attacking them constantly supported by strong artillery.

Krüger pointing with his *Ia*, Küchle, in the foreground.

The *Kampfgruppe* fended off every attack and inflicted heavy losses on the enemy until they were relieved after 16 days. In these crucial hours the *Obergruppenführer* remained unfailingly with the fighting troops, fearing no long marches through uncertain terrain, and through the fullest commitment of his own person he made sure that all difficulties which were encountered during the attacks as in the supply of the surrounded *Kampfgruppe* were solved in the shortest possible time. The relief of the surrounded *Kampfgruppe*, the *Geb.Jäg.Brigade 139*, was subordinated to the Division by the Gen.Kdo. Foreseeing the attack to relieve the *Kampfgruppe*, the enemy had [set up in] defensive positions on the isthmus Ssennosero -Wikssosero. On 14.06.1944, the *Brigade 139* set out to attack the Hill 150 which dominated the isthmus. The attack failed. Despite the concerns raised by the *Brigadekommandeur*, after rearranging the formations, the *Obergruppenführer* sent the Brigade back to attack again and, through close personal contact with the attacking troops, on the 16.07.1944 the hill 150 was captured. The success of the attack was only possible while the *Obergruppenführer* imposed his unconditional will upon the *Brigadekommandeur* to break through. After this initial success the Brigade remained, with 3 Btl. side by side facing towards the northwest along the bank of the western extension of the Ssennosero lake, without finding the necessary momentum to reach Ssennosero and push the enemy back towards the north. Only after having been pushed forward by the *Div. Kommandeur* was it possible to free the last parts of the surrounded *Kampfgruppe* and expel the enemy. With this the relief of the surrounded *Kampfgruppe* was completed and the enemy's intention of advancing to the south or the west via Ssennosero was thwarted.

Autumn 1944: Friedrich-Wilhelm Krüger after receiving the *Ritterkreuz* (30.09.1944) (*Marc Rikmenspoel*).

The decisive act:

1. Stopping the advance of the enemy on the isthmus Jeletjesero-Ssennosero.

2. Forcing the attack against Hill 150 despite the concerns raised by the *Brigadekommandeur*.

3. Deployment of the *Brigade 139* in a tight formation along the bank of the Ssennosero Lake.

Leadership merit:

1. A quick introduction of his own forces through a ruthless exposure of quieter sections of the front on the isthmus Jeletjesero -Ssennosero. Immediate action to attack an enemy force which itself was preparing to attack, inflicting such severe losses on the enemy force that it was no longer in a position to carry out an attack in that area, thereby freeing up new resources for immediate deployment to other parts of the front.

2. A timely deployment of Kampfgruppe Lapp in the area of the village of Ssennosero which resulted in extensive disruption of enemy intentions.

3. Securing the supply to the surrounded Kampfgruppe by air and water despite excessive enemy activity.

4. Gathering together all available forces for road building activities by combing through all the supply lines and service units, being well aware that a well-developed road network was a requirement in conducting successful warfare in forests und marshland.

5. Stability, decisiveness unimpressed by the numerical superiority of the enemy, with extreme daring and complete trust in the superiority of his own division. What was decisive was the fact that it was possible for the *Obergruppenführer* to mobilize a division which had been static for 2 years, to make it mentally and emotionally mobile and to yank them forwards to attack.

Achievement:
Through active combat, the enemy suffered massive losses, one division destroyed, a further division heavily weakened. Thereby thwarting the enemy's intention to surround the forces of the XVIII (Geb.) A.K. in the Louchi sector. An enemy success would have led to a complete collapse of the front in the Louchi sector, the possibility to reclaim the front would have been in question.

Enemy losses:
2157 enemy dead counted.
Estimated 3000 enemy dead.

Estimated 4000 enemy wounded.
(Source: SS-Personalakte of Friedrich-Wilhelm Krüger. Translation by Gary Costello)

25.04.1918: *Ritterkreuz des Kgl. Hausordens von Hohenzollern mit Schwertern*
15.05.1944: *1939 Spange zum 1914 Eisernes Kreuz I. Klasse* (awarded by Himmler for service with *7. SS-Freiwilligen-Gebirgs-Division "Prinz Eugen"*)
02.08.1943: *1939 Spange zum 1914 Eisernes Kreuz II. Klasse*
17.02.1915: *1914 Eisernes Kreuz I. Klasse* (per his own account, 03.02.1915)
07.09.1914: *1914 Eisernes Kreuz II. Klasse*
20.04.1942: *Kriegsverdienstkreuz I. Klasse mit Schwertern*
20.04.1942: *Kriegsverdienstkreuz II. Klasse mit Schwertern*
00.00.1917: *Österreichisches Militär-Verdienstkreuz III. Klasse mit Kriegsdekoration*
00.00.1918: *Verwundetenabzeichen, 1918 in Silber*
ca. 1920: *Verdienstabzeichen der II. Marinebrigade Wilhelmshaven, 1920, Schnalle*
00.00.19__: *Freikorpsabzeichen von Lützow (Erinnerungszeichen)*
00.00.1939: *Medaille zur Erinnerung an den 1. Oktober 1938*
ca. 1938: *Medaille zur Erinnerung an den 13. März 1938*
ca. 1934: *Ehrenkreuz des Weltkrieges 1914-1918 mit Schwertern*
30.01.1939: *Goldenes Ehrenzeichen der NSDAP*
ca. 1942: *Dienstauszeichnung der NSDAP in Silber*
00.00.1940: *Dienstauszeichnung der NSDAP in Bronze*
00.00.193_: *SS-Dienstauszeichnung 2. Stufe*
00.00.19__: *Polizeidienstauszeichnung 1. Stufe (Gold)*
00.00.193_: *Polizeidienstauszeichnung 2. Stufe (Silber)*
00.00.1940: *Ehrenzeichen für Deutsche Volkspflege 2. Stufe*
00.00.1937: *Deutsches Olympia-Ehrenzeichen II. Klasse*
00.00.1934: *SA-Sportabzeichen (Seesport) in Gold*
00.00.193_: *Deutsches Reiterabzeichen in Silber*
00.00.193_: *Ehrendegen des Reichsführers-SS*
00.00.193_: *Totenkopfring der SS*
00.00.193_: *SS-Zivilabzeichen(Nr. 17)*
16.12.1935: *Julleuchter der SS*
00.02.1934: *Ehrenwinkel für alte Kämpfer*
00.00.1938: Commemorative Medal of the War of 1914-1918 with Swords (Hungary)
00.01.1940: Grande Ufficiale dell'Ordine della Corona d'Italia (Grand Officer's Cross of the Order of the Crown of Italy)
00.00.1944: Order of the Iron Trefoil, 1st Class (Nezavisna Drzava Hrvatska [NDH, Independent State of Croatia])
00.00.1940: Order of Merit 1st Class (with Crown and Swords?) (Bulgaria)
00.05.1939: Order of the Crown of Yugoslavia 2nd Class with Star

Notes

* One of three sons of the later *Oberst* Alfred Gustav Krüger, killed in action near Liège (Ger.: Lüttich) on 06.08.1914 while commanding the Halberstadt-based *Infanterie-Regiment "Prinz Louis Ferdinand von Preußen" Nr. 27* (subordinated to *Generalmajor* Friedrich von Wussow's *14. Infanterie-Brigade*) and his wife Helene, née Glünder (died 00.00.1930). Younger brother of *SS-Obergruppenführer und General der Waffen-SS* Walter Krüger.

* Religion: Protestant until 00.00.193_, then left the church and declared himself *"deutschgläubig"*.

* Married on 16.09.1922 to Elisabeth Rasehorn (born 15.11.1896 in Bad Lausigk; NSDAP-Nr. 1 066 106; member of *NS-Frauenschaft* and *NS-Volkswohlfahrt*. Three children, including two sons (born 1929 and 1936), were born to this marriage.

Sources

Harrison, Jonathan; Mühlenkamp, Roberto; Myers, Jason; Romanov, Sergey; & Terry, Nicholas, "*Belzec, Sobibor, Treblinka. Holocaust Denial and Operation Reinhard. A Critique of the Falsehoods of Mattogno, Graf and Kues*", Holocaust Controversies, 2011.
Höhne, Heinz, "*The Order of the Death's Head*", Martin Secker & Warburg, 1969.
Mehner, Kurt (ed), "*Die Waffen-SS und Polizei 1939-1945: Führung und Truppe*", Militair-Verlag Klaus D. Patzwall, 1995.
Miller, Michael D. and Schulz, Andreas, "*Leaders of the SS & German Police, Volume 2 (Reichsführer-SS – SS-Gruppenführer; Hans Haltermann to Walter Krüger)*", R. James Bender Publishing, 2015.
National Archives and Records Administration, College Park, Maryland: SS-Personalakte of Friedrich-Wilhelm Krüger. Microfilm document collection A3343SS.
Office of United States Chief Counsel for Prosecution of Axis Criminality: Nazi Conspiracy and Aggression (11 volumes). U.S. Government Printing Office, District of Columbia, 1946.
Schulz, Andreas & Zinke, Dr. Dieter, "*Die Generale der Waffen-SS und der Polizei 1933-1945, Band 2 (Hachtel-Kutschera)*", Biblio-Verlag, 2005.
SS-Personalkanzlei and SS-Personalhauptamt: Dienstaltersliste der Schutzstaffel der NSDAP, Stand vom 1. Oktober 1934.
- Dienstaltersliste der Schutzstaffel der NSDAP, Stand vom 1. Juli 1935.
- Dienstaltersliste der Schutzstaffel der NSDAP, Stand vom 1. Dezember 1936.
- Dienstaltersliste der Schutzstaffel der NSDAP, Stand vom 1. Dezember 1937.
- Dienstaltersliste der Schutzstaffel der NSDAP, Stand vom 1. Dezember 1938.
- Dienstaltersliste der Schutzstaffel der NSDAP, Stand vom 30. Januar 1942.
- Dienstaltersliste der Schutzstaffel der NSDAP, Stand vom 20. April 1942.
- Dienstaltersliste der Schutzstaffel der NSDAP, Stand vom 9. November 1944.
Thomas, Franz & Wegmann, Günter, "*Die Ritterkreuzträger der Deutschen Wehrmacht. Teil VI: Gebirgstruppe. Band 1: A-K*", Biblio Verlag, 1993.
Williams, Max, "*SS Elite, Volume 2 (K-Q)*", Fonthill, 2017.
Witte, Peter (ed), et al, "*Der Dienstkalender Heinrich Himmlers 1941/42*", Christians, 1999.
Yahil, Leni, "*The Holocaust*", Oxford University Press, 1990.
Yerger, Mark C., "*Allgemeine-SS: The Commands, Units, and Leaders of the General SS*", Schiffer Military History, 1997.
Yerger, Mark C., "*Waffen-SS Commanders: Krüger to Zimmermann*", Schiffer Military History, 1999.

Addenda to Part 1 (Walter Krüger)

Career
Entry for 11.04.1941-15.11.1941: Omit "Succeeded Karl Maria Demelhuber. Succeeded by Richard Herrmann."

Notes
* One of three sons of the later *Oberst* Alfred Gustav Krüger, killed in action near Liège (Ger.: Lüttich) on 06.08.1914 while commanding the Halberstadt-based *Infanterie-Regiment "Prinz Louis Ferdinand von Preußen" Nr. 27* (subordinated to *Generalmajor* Friedrich von Wussow's *14. Infanterie-Brigade*) and his wife Helene, née Glünder (died 00.00.1930). Older brother of *SS-Obergruppenführer und General der Waffen-SS und Polizei* Friedrich-Wilhelm Krüger. This author has thus far been unable to locate any specific data regarding the third Krüger brother, however it is known from photographic evidence that he was also an army officer and recipient of the Iron Cross First Class.

* Religion: Protestant.

* Married on 18.05.1923 to Elenore ("Elli") Gerhardt (born 12.04.1897 in Posen; daughter of the then *Oberbürgermeister* of Halberstadt/Mecklenburg); member of the *NS-Frauenschaft* and *NS-Volkswohlfahrt*. One son (Gerhard, born 07.07.1927; member of *Hitler-Jugend*; possible service with *1. SS-Panzer-Division "Leibstandarte-SS Adolf Hitler"* [per Heinz Höhne]) and two daughters (Elisabeth, born 25.05.1924 and ____, born 06.07.1925; both served in the BDM).

«While I can walk, I will stay»
Awarded foreign DRK-nurses
by Samcevich Andrei

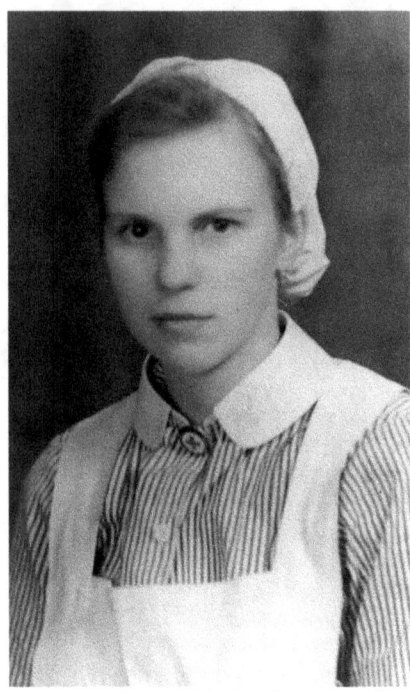

Young DRK-Helferin in everyday uniform (*Author`s collection*).

DRK-nurse on a German postcard from the World War II period.

Medical service is one of most important components of the war machine of any state both in peacetime and during the war. Women's military service has a long history. One could remember the legendary British nurse of the Crimean war Florence Nightingale. However, it dramatically enhanced in almost all participating countries during World War II. Germany was no exception in this regard – according to the Act of December 9, 1937, during the war, women replaced male staff and served in medical institutions of the armed forces. In addition to the uniform they received a personal identification mark of the pattern established by the Supreme Command of the *Wehrmacht*, an ID (*Verwendungsbuch*) – an analogue of the service record book – and an armband conforming to Geneva Convention standards. They served in hospitals (*Lazarett*), convalescent homes and sanitary trains at the established rate of working time of 60 hours a week, which often failed to be observed at the active combat zone. All kinds of troops of the German army and *Waffen-SS* had their hospitals with military medical personnel (doctors and orderlies), but the entire staff of nurses (*Schwester*) and nurse helpers (*Schwester-helferin*) (girls, who voluntarily joined the service during the war) was listed exclusively as part of the non-military organization of the German Red Cross (*Deutsches Rotes Kreuz*, DRK).

There was no doubt that the presence of woman in the military environment became the field of increased focus of soldiers, which often led to awkward or bewildering situations. For example, the Dutch SS volunteer Hendrik Verton later ironically described the procedure of disinfection of newcomers in the hospital: «*We were a living conveyor-belt for the «carbolic angels», the nurses who were ready to smear every hair-covered part of us with a disinfectant oil. It caused problems for those who had not seen a member of the female species in months. They were then the centre of teasing, grins, laughter and comments from their comrades, which the nurses diplomatically ignored, carrying out their duty with a faint smile on their lips».*

DRK-nurse on the German War Period Magazine.

DRK-nurse and German soldier returning from British captivity, Oktober 29, 1943.

DRK-nurses (*Author`s collection*).

The veteran of the 6th mountain division of the *Waffen-SS «Nord»* Johann Voss also later recalled: «*Afterwards, sitting there* [in the «Soldier`s house» – A.S.] *and smoking, I watched two Red Cross nurses working at the bar and cheerfully talking to the soldiers. Just to see real young women and to hear their soft voices plunged me into an inner turmoil. I hadn`t been near any females for a long time out there. I sat in my flecked combat blouse and my not-so-clean trousers. Watching them in their immaculate, light-gray dresses with the white aprons and collars, and a midst the general tidiness of the place, I began to understand what Heinrich had warned me of – I felt out of place. When one of the nurses passed by my seat, so closely that she brushed my face with her dress, I was thrown into complete confusion. I quickly got up and fled into the cinema».*

The absence of weapons and military status did not save the girls from all the horrors of war. On an equal footing with men they found themselves in the thick of the shooting war at the front, during the attacks of guerrillas and insurgents, air raids, and suffered heavy losses. For example, on February 11, 1943 the Soviet 4th guard tank corps unexpectedly captured the important town Krasnoarmeyskoye in the current Donetsk region of Ukraine. Before 19 February, the town was recaptured by the German troops and the Soviet penetration was wiped out, the Red Army soldiers had killed more than 600 prisoners there, including DRK-nurses and signal service *Helferin*.

DRK-nurses with soldiers, including Spanish volunteers from the «*Blue*» division.

DRK-flag raising ceremony.

As a result of an immediate military judicial investigation, according to incomplete statistics, the bodies of 406 German, 89 Italian, nine Romanian, four Hungarian, eight Ukrainian soldiers, 58 employees of the Organization Todt, 15 railway man and seven German civilians were identified. The investigation report says that all the corpses were naked, almost all the bodies were mutilated, many had their noses and ears cut off, others had their genitals cut off and stuffed into their mouths. As regards the murdered Red Cross nurses, an attempt was made to cut off their breasts «*in a brutal way*». According to the testimony of the captured commander of the anti-aircraft battery of the 14th guard tank brigade, Lieutenant Sorokin, the political Department of this brigade and in particular its commander, guard *Podpolkovnik* (Lieutenant Colonel) Vasily Shibankov, killed on February

19, 1943, had to bear the responsibility fort his crime. According to the official Soviet data, during the eight days of the city fighting 612 prisoners were captured (501 of which were taken captive on 11 February). This is probably the exact number of the killed.

Three Norwegian front-line sisters on destroyed Soviet *KV-2* tank.

Dutch DRK-nurse.

There were many similar episodes on the Eastern Front. For example, during the fighting in Budapest, in the captured German military hospital in the building of the current Széchényi library, not only did the Soviet soldiers search for Russian and Ukrainian volunteers of the *Wehrmacht* and *Waffen-SS* among the wounded, killing anyone who could not answer in German and throwing hand grenades into the wards, but also raped and stabbed several nurses. The massive recruitment of foreign volunteers from the occupied, allied and neutral countries, characteristic of Germany during the World War II, affected not only men but also women and girls. In particular, several thousands Norwegian, Dutch, Flemish, Danish, Walloon, French, Spanish, Ukrainian, Russian, Latvian, Estonian nurses joined the ranks of the DRK. Along with their German colleagues, they made a significant contribution to the overall military efforts of Germany, which was reflected in a significant numbers of awards of the Reich received by them.

Anna Gunhild Moxnes (centre) with two another Norwegian nurses.

Foreign nurses awarded the Iron Cross Class II

Front-line sister Anna G. Moxnes.

The DRK owed one of its largest contingents of nurses to Norway, where such girls (as well as in neighboring Denmark) were called «*front-line sisters*» (*Frontsøstre*). Some research estimate the number of Norwegian nurses at 350-450 people. But the data provided by the Norwegian specialist Anders Gogstad, according to which their number could have reached 500, seems more credible. He also writes that 432 Norwegian «front-line sisters» are known by the names (according to the information of the former *SS-Rottenführer* Knut Baardseth from *Panzer-Grenadier-Regiment 23 «Norge»*). 21 of them were killed in action and one – Anna Gunhild Moxnes (born November 9, 1914 in Narvik) – received the Iron Cross class II, becoming the first foreign woman, awarded with this cross. She was one of the first Norwegian nurses, who went to the Eastern Front in the first half of 1942. Besides her the group included Magndhild Fierli («*Maxi*»), Martha Eliassen («*Pin*»), Bertha Gulliksen, Yergine Felling, Wanda Corvedoff, Magna Sciacermo, Signe Hoel, Greta Stolz, Ruth Hoel,

Magnhild Langfeldt, Gudrun Herigstad, Elsa Stendal, Ragna Helene Voss, Elsa Kirkeby, Gerd Elvebakken («*Babs*»), Ingrid Engeness, Ester Recke, Grete Braaten, Mari Wilhelmsen, Inger Aune, Wenche Warendorph. Later Ragnhild Spokeli and Sonja Krei joined them in Kislovodsk, and Bjerg Lillian Frossli, Martha Sandli, Grette Gassman (missing in action in 1945), Karen Inga Hoffgard Budde (killing in action near Leningrad) – in Marienbad.

The honorary Badge of the front soldier (*Frontkjempermerket*).

Anna Gunhild Moxnes (centre) with the students of the Tronheim nursing school, 1966 (*Tronheim municipality*).

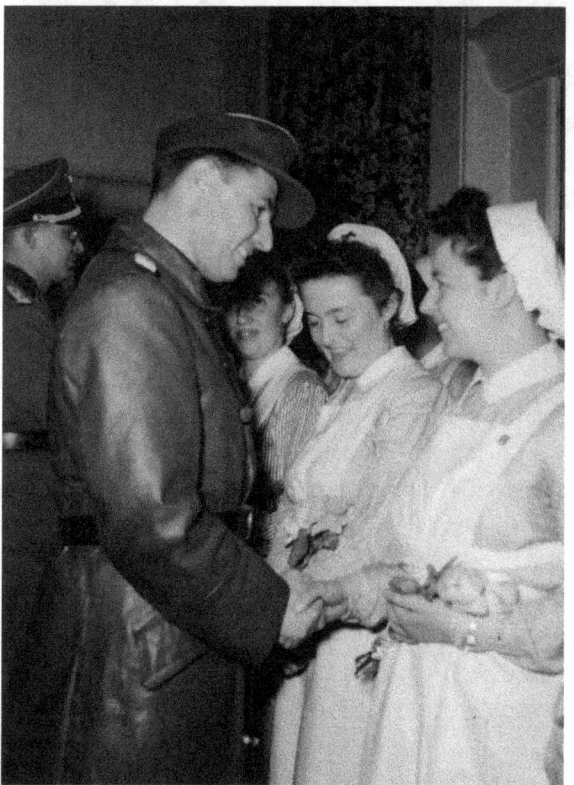

Léon Degrelle with Walloon nurses.

At first, Anna served in the hospital of the SS division «Wiking», including the offensive in the Caucasus. She consistently served in hospitals in Dnepropetrovsk, Kislovodsk, Bavarian Ruhpolding, hospital of the III SS Tank corps (*SS Korpslazarett 1/103*) in Marienbad and Tallinn, at the end of the war, in Pomeranian Hammerstein. She was awarded the Iron Cross for her bravery during a Soviet air raid on Tallinn on the night of 9-10 March 1944: at the risk of her life, Moxnes kept carrying the wounded soldiers out of the burning building all night, dressed only in nightgown and boots. In addition, the Norwegian government awarded the nurse the honorary Badge of the front soldier (*Frontkjempermerket*), which was awarded to her in Oslo on 15 September 1944, and the Badge of the front sister (*Frontsøstremerket*). After the war, Moxnes was sentenced to 15 months in prison for service on the Eastern front and three years for membership in the Norwegian national-socialist party National Unity. After the liberation in 1949, she was hardly able to get a job in Uleval hospital in Trondheim. Later she was the rector and the first teacher of the nursing school in Trondheim. The school graduates remembered her as an honest, very simple, serious, direct, smart and sportive woman. Moxnes was proud of their success; she had never started a family and had no children. Speaking about the past, she didn`t regret anything or renounce her views. She died in 1994 at the age of 80.

Norwegian nurses from the first contingent (NARA).

Young Walloon DRK-Helferin.

Unfortunately, we don`t know the name of another foreign nurse who received the Iron Cross II class. The former commander 28th volunteer Grenadier division SS «Wallonien» *SS-Standartenführer* Léon Degrelle writes about her. During the fierce fighting for the Stettin in Pomerania in March 1945, this Wallon nurse, already being a widow, lost her three sons. However, she asked Degrelle not to send her to the rear, but leave on the battlefield, where her children had died. As a result, delivering medical support to the wounded under the Soviet fire, she earned the Iron Cross.

The defense of the Silesian city of Breslau was extremely fierce and tenacious. Despite constant assaults from February 1945 till the end of the war, Soviet troops failed to break the resistance of the blocked German garrison, which was many times inferior to them in personnel and equipment and experienced logistical challenges. The commandant of the Breslau Fortress, *General* Hermann Niehoff, described the conditions under which the hospitals staff had to work: «*Staying in poorly ventilated bunkers-hospitals was a torment. Many of the wounded died from lack of fresh air.*

General **Hermann Niehoff.**

German soldiers in Breslau, 1945.

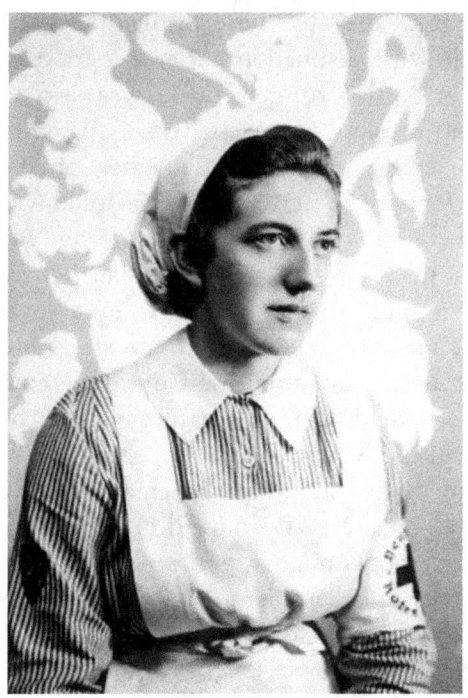

Flemish DRK-nurse.

By the time of the capitulation of the fortress, the number of badly wounded soldiers had reached about 10.000». During the defense, several DRK-nurses were awarded Iron Cross II class. Among them were at least two foreign women. The first was «*young and blonde*» *Helferin* Lillian Sorensen, a 19-year-old Danish girl from Copenhagen. She arrived in Germany in the autumn of 1943 to work in agriculture as part of the «*Land Service*» of Hitler Youth. In the next July, Lillian signed up for the DRK because, in her own words, «*her only wish was to help the soldiers*». A few months later she was sent from Cuxhaven to Breslau, where she arrived on December 21, 1944. There, the young Danish woman expressed a desire to serve on the front line in one of the battalions defending the city. Serving in its ranks under the Soviet artillery and mortar fire the girl did her best, and on February 26, 1945 received a through wound by the splinter of a mortar shell which flew through a window to the cellar, where she was. However, after being rendered assistance, she refused admission to hospital, saying later to a war correspondent Hans-Joachim Herzog: «*While I can walk, I will stay*». In addition to the Iron Cross II class, Sorensen also received the Wound Badge (probably the Black one).

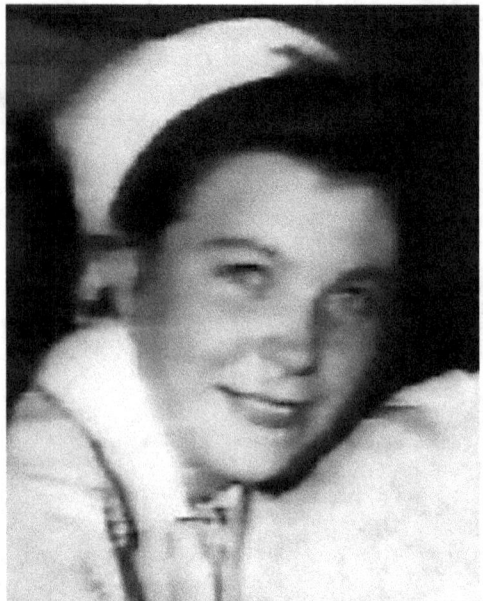

DRK-Helferin **Lucie Lefever.**

General-Major **Hans von Ahlfen.**

Soviet artillery in action at Breslau.

A Flemish girl, Lucie Lefever, born on September 7, 1925 in the town of Elverding near Ypres and joining the DRK in August 1943 (living at that time in Brillen, Veurnstraat, 158), became the second foreign nurse awarded the Iron Cross for the defense of Breslau. In the post-war documents of the Belgian judiciary, she is named Lucien (full name is Lucien Maria Cornelia), but in this paper we are going to use the «Lucie» variant found in most of the sources known to us. Lefever was born in a patriotic Flemish family and was a member of the national-socialist youth organization the Union of Dutch Girls. This explains her dream of serving as a nurse at the Eastern Front. She spent three months training in Thuringia. Due to her illness, she missed the exam and took it separately from other Flemish girls together with German nurses. But, despite these difficulties, she passed it with distinction. After a period of service in Bad Salzungen, Lucie was sent to Lissa near Breslau, where she was assigned to a pharmacy. As remembered by her, on the night of January 20-21, 1945, their hospital was alarmed and they were evacuated from the front line to Klein Bessa near Breslau, where they were put up for the night in a local school. The next day, they were transferred to Griffin Castle, 1 km from the Oder, where an improvised field hospital was organised. The number of the wounded was huge, they were placed in the corridors and basement, having to be laid on the straw due to lack of beds. There were not enough supplies of medicines, instruments and bandages. The hospital was dislocated in the castle until February 17, when, due to the narrowing of the stronghold, they were transferred nearer to the center of the city, into a building non-adapted for this purpose. The wounded were transported on horse-drawn carts. For a long time, the garrison managed to keep the airfield, which was captured by the Red Army only on Easter Monday, April 11th. On the way back, the planes took the wounded, civilians and those on marching orders. Thus, from February 15 to March 27, 3692 wounded (apart from those taken out on March 23 and 27), 123 able-bodied soldiers and officers (including *General-Major* Hans von Ahlfen), 230 civilians and three couriers were evacuated from the city. Badly wounded soldiers should have been accompanied by nurses under age.

SS-Ostuf. Besslein.

Hall of the Century complex in Breslau.

Delegation of German officers walking to negotiations for capitulation of Festung Breslau.

The destroyed Cathedral of Breslau, 1945.

However, as Lefever remembers: «*I don't believe that among us there were those who considered is possible to leave their patients*», so the girls tried to dismiss this opportunity, with each flight dreaming that someone else would fly. The medical unit, in which besides Lucie a doctor and several other nurses served, was a part of the fortress regiment of the *SS-Ostubaf.* Georg Robert Besslein. Constantly being under fire, it repeatedly changed its places of deployment, the last of which was the «*Hall of the Century*» complex. The work practically did not stop –if the nurses did not deal directly with the wounded, they were in the kitchen or in the laundry room, sterilizing bandages and medical instruments. Service under these conditions brought Lucie the Iron Cross II class, which she was presented on March 10, 1945 at the command post of the regiment by *Ostubaf.* Besslein.

Flemish DRK-nurse (ADVN, F199).

Flemish politician active August Borms with the Flemish DRK-nurses (ADVN, VFB 1093).

Appearing at 20.00 on May 5, the message about the capitulation of the garrison dismayed the girl's colleagues: «*The whole hell was nothing compared to this death sentence*». Lefever, another Dutch nurse, a dentist, a Flemish orderly, and several lightly wounded men decided not to surrender and try to get out of the city. They walked for two nights, hiding in ruins during the day, but on the second or third evening they encountered a Soviet patrol and were captured. Until 22:00 of the next day, they continuously moved in a column of POWs in an unknown direction. The guards killed everyone who was behind or could not walk. So many elderly *Volkssturmmann* were lost. Until August 1945, Lucie was in concentration camp, working in the field and undergoing beatings and violence, when she was spotted by a Soviet female officer, for whom the Flemish nurse made a dress, for which the latter received extra messing. Then she, along with other foreigners, was sent by train to Magdeburg, where they were exchanged for Soviet POWs arriving from the West. The Soviet POWs, unwilling to return to the USSR, stubbornly resisted, holding hands, and the guards had to drag them away by force. The arrivals were distributed to national camps (the Flemish were in the Belgian one) and after a three-week stay there they were sent to Belgium, where, according to Lefevre, «*our «home» again meant captivity*». After the war in the homeland, the girl was convicted twice for serving in the DRK: on June 11, 1946, she was sentenced to nine months in prison and five years of police supervision, and on January 24, 1950, to the deprivation of right to the extent provided for in Art. 123 of the Belgian Criminal Code (deprivation of all voting rights, the right to work in the legal and educational fields, to participate in political newspaper activities and the creation of any cultural products that pursue political goals, the right to head political associations and hold unpaid positions in public and trade union organizations, to hold a state-paid position of a priest). Shortly after being released from prison, Lucie married *Nationalsozialistisches Kraftfahrkorps* (NSKK) veteran Romeo Lejeune (born September 9, 1921, died in Vatu in December 1987). She held the post of Public Relations Advisor at the Center of the former volunteers of the Eastern Front of Flanders. In addition, for 10 years she was engaged in teaching lace making, the work of her apprentice being repeatedly exhibited. A historian Johan Trigg writes about Lefever: «Today Lucie is a lively lady with neatly cut hair and a strong but friendly handshake. She is petite, but her blue eyes are still very bright».

DRK-Helferin Martha Clement (*W. Winkeler*).

Barracks of the SS-Division *Leibstandarte Adolf Hitler*, in the Berlin-Lichterfelde district.

Flemish *Waffen-SS* frontline nurses.

Actually, the northern part of Belgium – Dutch-speaking Flanders – gave the DRK the largest contingent of nurses among all European countries. A total of about 600 Flemish women (mostly unmarried) served in hospitals in Germany and other European countries. Their average age ranged from 18 to 25. At least one more of them was also awarded the Iron Cross II class, having received it for the last fights in Berlin in April 1945. It was Martha Clement, born January 18, 1922 in Antwerp, joining the DRK in 1944. According to her memoir, on April 21, 1945, Walloon and Flemish *DRK-helfers* and NSKK-men were assembled in the barracks of the SS division «Leibstandarte» in the Lichterfelde district of Berlin. Among the former, Martha knew only a Flemish man Theo Van Reek (in Berlin he was wounded in the face, after the war he lived in Belgian Vilreike), and among the latter – Jos Op`t Eynde, also her countryman. The improvised hospital formed in the barracks consisted, in addition, of a Walloon *SS-Sturmbannführer* Dr. Jacqmain, whose work under extremely limited resources Clement admired, and three nurses: Martha herself, a Flemish woman Monica Clootens from Bergen and a Dutch woman Leni. Due to the constant shelling, 180 wounded people, including those in critical condition, were placed in the basement. There were no anesthetic, bandages or medications. The staff could only give out cognac to patients three times a day, the stock of which they had found in the barracks. There were also a few bags of semolina, which, diluted with water, was theirs taple diet. They were tearing sheets from a laundry room, which they forced open, to make bandages. On April 28, the girls received an order from Dr. Jacqmain to leave the barracks. However, they refused to perform it and abandon the wounded. Eventually, it was decided to draw lots, and Monica Clootens would have to stay. The two other sisters and about 40 wounded soldiers able to walk, splitting into groups of four, began to get out of Berlin. Martha managed to do it and, accompanying the SS soldier Richard Richter, she was able to get to Flensburg, where they surrendered to the Americans. Later, Richter wrote Clement, but she, while imprisoned in Vilvoorde, could not write back. As she learned later, during the capture of the barracks, Soviet soldiers killed all the wounded there. The fate of Monica Clootens remained unknown – the post-war requests of her parents did not bring results. Dr. Jacqmain, who had also stayed with his patients, was captured by the Soviet army, though he managed to escape, but was re-captured by US troops and spent a long time in Belgian prisons. After his release he lived in Erlangen (Germany). Among the wounded, Martha saw another Flemish man, whose nationality she identified by an armband with a lion; an 18-19-year-old blond man. He had a severe head wound, and he did not regain consciousness. There was no personal identification mark on him, but he wore a small icon on a black cord around his neck, and a silver wedding ring on his finger. The former nurse Martha Clement died on April 14, 1982 at the age of 60.

Kriegsverdienstkreuz II Klasse mit Schwertern.

Foreign nurses awarded with the War Merit Cross and with the War Merit Medal

The War Merit Cross (German: *Kriegsverdienstkreuz*), instituted on October 18, 1939, in two classes and in the variants with and without swords, and the medal of this order (German: *Kriegsverdienstmedaille*), introduced into the award system of Germany in August 1940, were less honorable, but much more common that the Iron Cross award. They were awarded for a wide range of military merits, including the performance of official duties under enemy fire and during air raids (in which case, the recipient received a cross with swords). All categories of citizens — soldiers, civilians, employees and members of paramilitary, political, public organizations, as well as foreign volunteers involved in the military and civil structures of the *Reich* — were to be awarded the order. The medal was awarded exclusively to civilians, including employees of industrial and agricultural enterprises, the DRK, *Helfers* and *Helferin* of the air defense support service. Often the award was given to foreign nurses, among whom was the Flemish Maria (full name – Maria Adriana Petronella) Van Aerden, born July 23, 1922 in the Netherlands Bergen op Zoom. This girl from Antwerp was one of the 25 first Flemish DRK-nurses who started taking a course at the Belgian Spa in January 1943. On February 5 they left for Germany to continue their education in three Hamburg hospitals.

Flemish propaganda postcard with Maria Van Aerden and Jules Geurts, the first Flemish volunteer to be awarded the Iron Cross I class for bravery.

Hilfsschwester Maria Van Aerden (*Wim Winkeler*).

Notably, the instruction program included not only the development of practical medical skills, but also ideological training. Maria was awarded the War Merit Cross II class with swords for doing the duty on the days of massive raids by Anglo-American aviation over Hamburg in August 1943: the hospital in which she served was set on fire, the nurses did their best to save the wounded, repeatedly returning to the fire. Concurrently, Van Aerden suffered from carbon dioxide poisoning. Having survived one of the most destructive airstrikes of war, the young Fleming died a few months later during the Soviet air raid over Tallinn on the night of March 9-10, 1944, while serving in the hospital of the III SS tank corps. Some circumstances of her death were described in the newspaper of the Flemish SS «*De SS-man*» (after the war, the article was reprinted in the veteran magazine «*Berkenkruis*»). According to another nurse – Agnes Van Dongen– Maria was doing the night shift, which she started at 18.45. When the hospital was hit by high-explosive and incendiary bombs and the fire broke out, all service-free sisters (including the recently replaced Van Dongen) rushed to extricate the wounded. One of the doctors already on the spot told her about the wounded Flemish nurse who remained in the building and, along with the others, Agnes rushed after her.

The War merit medal.

Hamburg in Ruins after Allied raid, Summer 1943.

Another Flemish propaganda postcard with Maria Van Aerden.

When they found Van Aerden, she was already unconscious and it was impossible to do anything – she died that day. The grave of Maria Van Aerden is located at the memorial cemetery of Maaryamäe in Tallinn (Estonia).

Born February 26, 1922 in Antwerp, Van Dongen (full name – Agnes-Joanna Van Dongen) was also awarded the Cross II class with swords. She began her service on March 9, 1943, leaving from Brussels to Spa with the group of 32 nurses, where she studied for three weeks at the DRK sanatorium, and on the 28th of the same month she left (together with 25 other girls) for Berlin. Upon the arrival at Potsdam Station, they were sent to continue their studies at the *Reichsführer* School in Gross-Schulzendorf, where they stayed until April 2, after which they were divided into groups and sent to internships in rear hospitals. Agnes was assigned to Augusta Hospital (Berlin, Scharnhorststrasse, 3). On July 1, the girls were again gathered together and sent to Piritz to take the exam, which took place six days later. As a result, only the 15 of them were enrolled in the staff of the DRK, having received *Schwestern-helferin* brooches, the rest went home, having shown unsatisfactory results. This was followed by the distribution: four Flemish women (including Hilde Dockx and Simone Labiau) returned to the Hindenburg Hospital in Berlin, as they were too young to be sent to the front; two more (Lisette Casse and Mia Struyf) had to take an additional month of practice, which they missed due to illness; Maria Beecman and another girl were assigned to Krakow, one girl was returned home as «*unsuitable for the work of a nurse*». Van Dongen and the other two helferins – Mitsi Dekker and Maria Van Zundert – were assigned to the hospital of the III SS Tank Corps, left for Marienbad on 10 July. There they had another three months of practice, following which they received the status of «assistant nurses» (*Hilfsschwester*) and the corresponding oblong brooches.

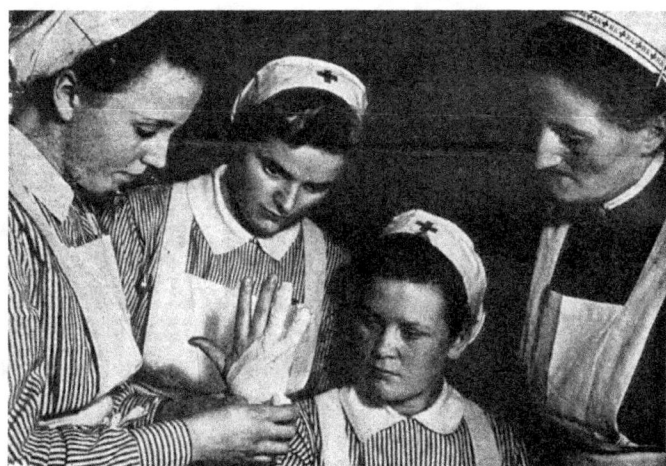

Training session for future Flemish DRK-nurses.

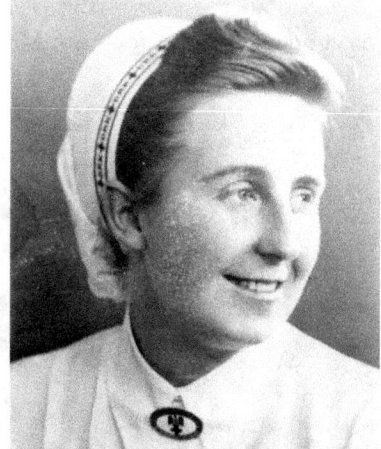

Agnes Van Dongen (*W.Winkeler*).

Anna Gunhild Moxnes, Agnes Van Dongen and unknown Norwegian nurse awarded the Cross for Military Merit (from left to right).

In October, all the three went on leaf to Flanders, from which Mitsi and Maria did not return to the infirmary for various reasons. The following month Van Dongen, along with the rest of the hospital staff, left for Croatia, where they were dislocated 120 km from Zagreb until January 1944, when they were transferred to the Eastern Front. Until February, Agnes served in the Hungerburg field hospital at Narva, then in Tallinn, where, as stated above, she survived a Soviet airstrike on March 9, after which until April the hospital of the III SS Tank Corps was in Harikula, and then in Volpere. Among the wounded, some Flemish volunteers were admitted to the hospital, one of whom – the *SS-Untersharführer* Jeff Van Houtven – left memories about Van Dongen: «*We were in the Volpere Infirmary in Estonia. They were joking the way you would* never joke among pastors. But when Schwester Agnes Van Dongen entered the room, everyone was speaking differently. And it was amazing. We didn`t ponder about it, but she created a distance between the ugly and the clean. Wherever she appeared – the line between pure and obscene appeared. She rode 150 km on hard snow with a courier in a wheelchair of his motorcycle, because she learned that a guy from Hoboken was dying in another hospital. Eighteen years old, and when he was given anti-tetanus, he said that he had probably already become infected. Now the convulsion was warping by the soldier`s body from the inside... The Flemish nurse still came in time to help him and cover his eyes». In September, the hospital of the III SS Tank Corps was evacuated by sea from Tallinn to Königsberg, after which it changed the places of dislocation in northern Germany several times until it settled in Nekhlin at Easter 1945. The end of the war found Van Dongen in Schwerin, in a hospital where she had been assigned shortly before. On May 2, she, along with the rest of the garrison, surrendered to American troops.

Left photo: Latvian nurses with a Latvian legion inspector *SS-Gruppenführer* Rūdolfs Bangerskis (stands third on the left). Fourth on the left — Alvīne Suna, sixth on the left – Erna Bomis. Right photo, Erna Bomis.

Alvīne Suna.

Another of the awardees was the Latvian nurse Alvīne Suna, who used to work in the 2nd Riga hospital. She served in various hospitals on the northern sector of the Eastern Front, in particular, in Pskov, and distinguished herself at the battles on the Volkhov front when the hospital located a few kilometers from the front line was under Soviet artillery fire and air raids. Suna was the first to notice an incendiary bomb hit the roof of a building and took steps to eliminate the danger. As a result, in the spring of 1944 she became the first awarded Latvian nurse, receiving a War Merit Cross II class with swords from the commander of the 19th Latvian SS division *SS-Oberführer* Bruno Streckenbach. In fact, in the beginning, Suna was granted the Iron Cross, but this decision was rejected, despite the consent of the German medical authorities.

Spanish nurses from the wartime magazine.

DRK-Helferin Ida Köhler (*T. Greiner Eggan*).

Perhaps the reason was the prejudice of some regional leaders of the SS had for the Latvians, primarily, the commander of the SS *Oberabschnitt* Ostland, *Obergruppenführer* SS Friedrich Ekkel, or the unwillingness to handout a higher award by gender.

On June 18, 1944, another Latvian nurse, Erna Bomis, received her Military Merit medal. In 1941 she graduated from the nursing school at the 2nd Riga hospital, and since April 1943 she served at the front. The decoration was also administered by *SS-Obf.* Bruno Streckenbach.

At the end of the war, on May 1, 1945, the Norwegian *DRK-Helferin* Ida Köhler (born August 9, 1916 in Hommelvik) from the 504th field hospital of the IV SS tank corps (who used to serve in the SS infirmary in Minsk) was awarded the War Merit medal. She received the medal only on June 24, 1945.

Foreign nurses awarded other medals and badges

The badge of distinction for the Easter nations for Bravery and for Merits (German: *Tapferkeits und Verdienstauszeichnung für Ostvölker*) were established on July 14, 1942 to award distinguished soldiers and officers of the «Eastern» (Russian, Ukrainian, Cossack, Baltic, Turkestan, Tatar and Caucasian) units of the German army, as well as civilian collaborators. There were five grades – bronze, silver and gold II class, as well as silver and gold I class, providing for consistent rewarding from lower to higher grades. The uniqueness of the award in the German award system was that in some cases the badges of higher degrees were granted, bypassing the lower ones. It`s known about the Russian nurse Olga Dolinskaya, awarded the silver badge for Bravery II class. This girl served on the sanitary train of 12 carriages, which departed on 12.15 August 24, 1944 from the Romanian station of Ploiesti and was attacked by the troops of Romania which went over to the side of the opponents of Germany: having covered 9 Km the train was stopped by tanks that had blocked the railway, and also came under artillery fire. 10 minutes later, the Romanian soldiers approached the carriages and began to rob the train and then set the carriages on fire.

Unknown Dutch nurse from the 504th field hospital of the IV SS tank corps awarded the Cross for Military Merit (*Tore Greiner Eggan*).

Silver badge of distinction for the Easter nations for Bravery II class.

At this point, Dolinskaya managed to leave the burning train and hide in the nearby forest, after which she alone headed to join the German troops at the Hungarian border. Later, a correspondent wrote: «*Days went by. Olya lost track of time. Her dress was torn, her shoes had long been abandoned. Occasionally daring to leave the forest, she dug up potatoes and ate them raw, not risking to make a fire. During the day, guided by the sun, at night by the stars, she walked west. There, to the Hungarian border. She often saw Soviet tanks pass along the road. She heard Soviet songs that her compatriots sang – the Russian people dressed in Red Army uniforms. They passed, their song faded away and then Olya risked crossing the road and again go deep into the forest*». As a result, she, already in a semi-unconscious state, managed to meet a group of 124 Russian *Wehrmacht* volunteers under the command of Lieutenant Shevchenko,

DRK medal «*For Caring for the German nation*».

Maria Cristina de Orive Alonso.

who, like her, had disentangled the for 10 days; it took them three more days to cross the front line.

The award system of the Third Reich was distinguished with extreme diversity, for instance, apart from state awards, there were departmental awards, which included the DRK medal «*For Caring for the German nation*», that was common among nurses. Foreign nurses also received it. Among them there were the Spanish women Maria Cristina de Orive Alonso and Dolores Bertran Seusa (formerly participants of the Spanish Civil War) from the IV reserve hospital of the 250th Spanish Volunteer («Blue») division of the *Wehrmacht*. The former was born in 1919 in Madrid and was a member of the women`s section of the far-right party Spanish Falange. In 1941, she (as well as Seusa) joined the first nursing contingent of the Blue division. Later, Maria said that she «*went to Russia because she had to accompany her party mates who left classes. To fight communism*». Until the summer of 1942, *Helferin* de Orive served in Porkhov and Königsberg, after which she returned to Spain. On returning, she continued to work as a nurse, and in 1946 she married Agustin Payno Mendicoague, a former orderly of the 1st anti-tank company of the 250th division. Nine children were born in this marriage. Maria Cristina died in the summer of 2012 at the age of 92 years. According to the necrology, she was known as «*a great lover of reading, plants, photography, working for the local parish*».

On October 3, 1942, the Norwegian newspaper *Fritt Folk* published an interview with the front sister Maria Ingebrygsen, which she gave during her three-week vacation for family reasons. Unlike most nurses of the first contingent sent to the southern sector of the Eastern Front, she belonged to a group of five, first assigned to Riga, and then to a front-line region of Army Group «North». Speaking about her colleagues – Anne-Maria Bjornstadt, Magnhild Langfeld, Wenke Warendorff and Grete Stoltz – Maria mentioned that the two latter were awarded the German «*medical award for brave behavior near Kirkines*». Probably, that entails the medal «*For Caring for the German nation*».

The Axis Forces

Eastern Front Medal.

Maria Monserrat Romeu.

The medal «*For the winter campaign in the East 1941-1942*» (The Eastern Front Medal, *Winterschlacht im Osten 1941/42* in German), received by military personnel and other persons who served at least two weeks directly in the line of the Eastern front or at least 60 days in a combat zone during the period from 15 November 1941 to 15 April 1942, was quite common among German nurses. But for foreigners, this award was rare because most of them were inducted into the DRK at a later date. But there were exceptions, for example, another Spanish woman from the first contingent of nurses of the «*Blue*» division – born October 14, 1915 in the Catalan Sant Sadurni d`Anoia Maria Monserrat Romeu («Monse»). Educated as a nurse at the University of Barcelona, on July 8, 1937, she entered the female section of the Spanish Phalanx and from after September 1938 took part in the Spanish Civil War on the side of the nationalists of General Franco, serving first at the General Mola hospital in San Sebastian and then at the Red Cross Military Hospital in Leganes. Together with other nurses enrolled in the Spanish division, Maria left Madrid at the end of August 1941 and headed for the east through Paris, Stuttgart, Nuremberg, Grafenvor and Berlin. Initially she served in the Spanish hospital in Warsaw, then – at the Eastern Front, in the German hospital in Smolensk, as well as in Spanish ones in Porkhov, Riga and Königsberg. Together with the rest of the nurses, she was demobilized on July 16, 1942. In June 1945, she married the veteran of the «*Blue*» division Juan Fernandez de Loasa, giving birth to eight children in this marriage. She died in Ronda in 2004. According to her personal book of the Spanish Auxiliary Military Medical Service, the participation in the Second World War brought her two awards: the Spanish Medal «For the Campaign in Russia» and the German medal, marked in a similar way (*Medalla de la Campaña de Rusia (alemana)*. In our opinion, that entails Medal «*For the Winter Campaign in the East 1941-1942*».

Bibliography

The author expresses his sincere gratitude for aid and material provided to Wim Winkeler (Belgium), Patrik Agte (Germany) and Tore Greiner Eggan (Norway).

Massimiliano Afiero, "*Norwegian Waffen-SS Legion, 1941-1943*", Osprey Publishing 2019
Author`s personal archive
«*Belgisch Staatsblad*», 1 november 1946.
«*Belgisch Staatsblad*», 19 juli 1950.
Blindheim S. "*Frontkjemperbevegelsen. Hovedoppgave i Historie*", Universitetet i Oslo, 1974.

Central Archive of the Ministry of Defense of the Russian Federation

Degrelle L., "*Campaing in Russia. The Waffen SS on the Eastern Front*", Institute for historical review, 1985.

DRK.-Schwestern – im Fronteinsatz bewährt / «*Znaimer Tagblatt*» №289, 7 dezember 1944.

Ein flämisches Mädchen mit EK 2 // «*Der Freiwillige*» №1, januar/februar 2013.

Fonn M., Hernæs N., Hofstad E. Hva skjedde med 1967-kullet? // «*Sykepleien*» №18, 6 desember 2007.

Fonn M. –*Unnskyld, frontsøstre!* // «*Sykepleien*» №3, 12 mars 2015.

Gogstad A. Gjemt eller glemt? Norske kvinner i tysk sanitetstjeneste under Den annen verdenskrig // «*Michael*» №5, 2008.

Gripp Bay E., "*Historien om frontsøstrene. De norske frontsøstrenes historie i et nytt lys. Masteroppgave i historie*", Universitetet i Oslo, November 2014.

Hvorfol svek du oss – Nøklebye Heiberg? Den første kontigent frontsøstre / «*Folk og Land*» №3, 1998.

Jacinto A. María Cristina de Orive, "*última enfermera de la División Azul*"/ «*El País*», 26 septiembre 2012.

Klietmann K.-G., "*Auszeichnungen des Deutschen Reiches 1936-1945*", Stuttgart, 2004.

Kriegsberichter Hansjoahim Herzog Dänische DRK.-Helferin erhielt das EK. 2 / «*Schlesischen Tageszeitung*» №71, 16 märz 1945.

Lumsden R., "*Medals and Decorations of Hitler`s Germany*", Shrewsbury, 2001.

Neulen H.W., "*An deutscher Seite. Internationale Freiwillige von Wehrmacht und Waffen-SS*", München, 1992.

Norske kvinner pleiet Hitlers soldater ved Østfronten. 70 år etter vekker innsatsen strid / «*Dagbladed*» http://www.skivebom.com/lastned/historie/frontsøstre_dagbladet_pluss.pdf

Peeters T., "*Het Sint-Maartensfonds. Een Vlaamse hulporganisatie en vereniging van voormalige vrijwilligers in nazi-Duitse (para-)militaire organisaties. Masterproef voorgedragen tot het behalen van de graad van Master in de Geschiedenis*", Universiteit Gent, 2013.

Querol C., *Onze mesos als fronts russos* / «*El 3 de vuit*», 16 abril 2010.

Schweizer J., *Les auxiliaries de la Deutsches Rotes Kreuz. Uniforme et équipement, 1938-1945* // «*Armes Militaria Magazine*» №314, septembre 2011.

Siemons S. *Sterren, die nooit tanen* // «*Berkenkruis*» №6, juni 1983.

SS kaŗa ziņotājs Graudulis R. Kaŗa nopelnu krusts latviešu māsai / «*Daugavas Vanagi*» №20, 19 maijs 1944.

Solarz J., "*Breslau 1945*", Warszawa, 2007.

Taylor H.P., *Vichinghi contro il bolscevismo. Il distintivo norvegese per I combattenti al fronte: il Frontkjempermerket* // «*Uniformi & Armi*» №164, dicembre 2009.

Tore Greiner Eggan personal archive.

Trigg J., "*Het testament van de Vlaamse Waffen-SS. De allerlaatste Oostfronters getuigen*", Antwerpen, 2017.

Ungváry K., "*Battle for Budapest. One Hundred Days in World War II*", London; New York, 2003.

Verton H., "*In the fire of the Eastern front: the experiences of a Dutch Waffen-SS Volunteer, 1941-45*", Mechanicsburg, 2010.

Vlaamsche DRK-Hilfsschwester met het KVK / «*Getrouwe Maldeghem*» №4, 23 januari 1944.

Vincx J.,"*Vlaanderen in uniform 1940-1945. Deel 2*", Antwerpen, 2004.

Vincx J., "*Vlamingen aan het Oostfront. Deel 2*", Antwerpen, 1975.

Voss J., "*Black Edelweiss. A Memoir of Combat and Conscience by a Soldier of the Waffen SS*", Bedford.

Vtrsserž. N. Uldriķa uzu. Apbalvojums latviešu māsai / «*Daugavas Vanagi*» №26, 30 jūnijs 1944.

Williamson G., "*World War II German Women's Auxiliary Services*", Oxford, 2003.

WW2 AXIS FORCES

www.ingramcontent.com/pod-product-compliance
Lightning Source LLC
LaVergne TN
LVHW081546070526
838199LV00057B/3793